Thames & Hudson

Robert O'Byrne

living in

DUBLIN

With 246 color photographs by

Alex Ramsay

CONTENTS

TO LIVE IN DUBLIN

Title pages *The Ha'penny Bridge.*

To Live in
DUBLIN
The City as a work in Progress

Unlike many other European capitals, Dublin is less a wise old lady than an unruly adolescent, still discovering her identity. Since the closing years of the 20th century, the city has been undergoing a transformation that has yet to be completed. In just a decade, her character and appearance have changed dramatically and it is not possible to discern what will be their eventual form.

Dublin's River Liffey: consistency through an era of change.

When James Joyce completed *Ulysses* in 1922 he claimed that, should such an undertaking ever become necessary, Dublin might be entirely rebuilt from the information on the city contained within his novel. Although it was almost twenty years since he had lived in Dublin, nevertheless his memories of its streets and squares continued to be vivid. And just as importantly, despite the detrimental effects of a rebellion against the British government, followed by a civil war, the physical nature of the city had remained very much as when he had left it in 1904 for what would prove to be permanent exile.

Were Joyce alive today, however, he would have to write another, much more substantial work, because in the intervening period Dublin had changed significantly. In *Ulysses* it is a relatively compact place and still predominantly contained within the canals that had encircled its boundaries since the late 18th century.

The city as a work of art. Paintings for sale on the railings of Merrion Square (above) and the rear of the State Apartments at Dublin Castle (right). The latter illustrates the gradual evolution of the city, with the 13th-century Record Tower flanked by the 19th-century Chapel Royal and the castle's 18th-century reception rooms.

The principal entrance to the upper courtyard of Dublin Castle was created in the mid-18th century (left). Notice how the figure of Justice above the gateway on the right has her back turned on the city.

Two of the most important monuments in the Phoenix Park, with that erected to the first Duke of Wellington (above left) at 205 feet being the largest obelisk in Europe. Begun in 1817 and designed by Robert Smirke, its plaques were cast from cannons captured at the Battle of Waterloo. Although a native of Dublin, Wellington seems not to have cared for the city, saying that just because a man was born in a stable, that did not make him a horse. Of an earlier date is the Phoenix Pillar (right), placed at the centre of the park in 1747 by the Lord Lieutenant of the time, the Earl of Chesterfield.

Today's Dublin has long broken free of man-made constraints and sprawls for miles to the north, south and west, only checked in its eastward spread by the Irish Sea.

In his entertaining memoirs written during the early years of the last century, the Irish novelist George Moore remarked, 'Dublin dwindles so beautifully; there is no harsh separation between it and the country; it fades away.' Such is still the case, although not necessarily in the manner proposed by Moore who, after all, only settled in the city for a decade. The Irish are suspicious of high-rise buildings, they like to live in their own homes; and compared with elsewhere in Europe, their country is sparsely populated. These factors, combined with an abundance of available land, means that at times Dublin can seem to meander deep into the surrounding countryside.

Ever since the early 1990s, the builder's crane has become a dominant presence on Dublin's skyline, forcefully reflecting the greatest economic transformation that the city – and indeed the whole of Ireland – has undergone for more than two centuries. The amount of people living in Dublin has more than tripled compared with numbers a hundred years ago. The city now holds around one-third of the entire Irish state's population, as towns and boroughs formerly with their own distinctive identities have become absorbed into the capital.

Inevitably, this expansion has had an effect on the Dublin recalled by Joyce and so many other writers before and since, for whom the place became a preoccupation. That 'air of mild melancholy' which architectural historian Maurice Craig believes first settled over the city in the mid-19th century remained as a distinctive presence for the next hundred years and more. And melancholy tended to encourage stasis among the citizenry of Dublin. At the time he was writing his book of short stories, *Dubliners*, Joyce described the city as being 'the centre of paralysis.' He may have regarded this characteristic with disapproval, but for other observers the sense of time suspended was what gave Dublin its special charm; while the rest of Europe moved relentlessly forward, here was a city where little

St Audoen's, the only surviving gate from the Norman walls of the city, dates from the 13th century (left). Harking back to the Middle Ages are these heads carved on the exterior of a police station at the start of the 20th century on Pearse Street (above). And from the golden age of the city (overleaf) are the beautifully preserved interiors of Charlemont House, one of the most important private residences built in Georgian Dublin to the designs of Sir William Chambers. Today it is home to the Municipal Gallery of Modern Art.

had changed within living memory. The only per[cep]tible alteration was that with each successive generatio[n] the houses became a little more weather-beaten, th[e] populace a touch shabbier, the pervasive mood slightly more melancholic.

Of late, the last vestiges of that Dublin have entirely disappeared, mourned perhaps by a few romantics hostile to change, but otherwise not greatly to be regretted. True, there have been casualties during the course of the city's recent transformation, both in terms of its appearance and character. The relaxed pace of life, slow sometimes to the point of stupor, which was once a feature of the Irish capital, has quite gone; living in Dublin can now be as demanding and frenetic as in any other large urban centre around the globe. And many of the Georgian buildings which were one of its most distinctive features have been demolished, replaced with more practical, if less overtly charming, structures. But it should not be overlooked that those 18th-century houses and terraces were often built on the sites of even older properties, the memory of which has been all but forgotten. As our less sentimental forebears would confirm, living cities demand a degree of ruthlessness from their inhabitants; otherwise they risk the fossilization from which Dublin suffered for so long.

For a place that used to give the impression of having settled comfortably into middle age, Dublin is actually a comparatively youthful development and the present appearance of its centre dates back little more than two centuries. Many of Europe's leading cities can trace their origins over several millennia. In the company of such ancient grandees, Dublin – like so many of its contemporary inhabitants – resembles an awkward adolescent, still unsure of its place and persona. The Irish temperament is traditionally not urban, which is why the country's capital can seem quite raw to outside observers and its citizens look as though they have yet to grow accustomed to their status.

Ireland's ancient people were tribal and nomadic, traits still visible in a caste of Irish society once known as 'tinkers' but now more usually called 'travellers'.

Perhaps these travellers are the only true descendants of the Celts who once occupied the entire island; after all, Ireland has been prey to a number of invasions, that of the Vikings being responsible for the establishment of the first urban settlements, including Dublin in the early 10th century. But its name derives from two Irish words *dubh linn*, meaning 'the black pool'.

Scarcely any trace of Viking Dublin now remains; even the core street system of the period was almost entirely obliterated in the late 20th century. Some eight hundred years earlier, the Anglo-Normans came to Ireland, and it was they who officially made Dublin the country's capital. Not that it could often claim that title over much of the island, large parts of which remained for several more centuries under the control of the native Irish. That they regarded Dublin with hostility can be seen by the development of a fortified area around the city to ensure the latter's security. This was called the Pale, from which derives the phrase 'beyond the pale.' Centuries of struggle for control of Ireland meant that by the mid-17th century, the burghers of Dublin could describe their city as devastated by 'the severall calamities of warrs, pestilence and famine'. Hence there is a lack of buildings in the city dating from much before 1700. The combination of assault by armies – English and Irish – and neglect due to money shortage meant that, in the 18th century, Dublin had to be almost entirely rebuilt. This opportunity was seized upon with relish and over the course of little more than a hundred years, the city was beautified as never before or since. The 18th century was Dublin's golden age. But the age closed and when, in 1800, the Act of Union was passed, permanently dissolving Ireland's independent parliament and ensuring that all legislation would henceforth be passed in London, the city began to slip into a period of decline as gradual as it was melancholy.

An arts and crafts interpretation of the Florentine palazzo, the Sunlight Chambers with its fine tiled friezes (left) stands on the corner of Essex Quay and Parliament Street. Around the corner in Temple Bar's Meeting House Square, a popular food market takes place every Saturday (right).

Although the 19th century was not the finest time for Dublin, nevertheless it left the city some remarkable buildings, including the delightful Natural History Museum dating from 1856 (above right) which looks as though nothing has changed inside since it was built. Constructed during the same decade, the Museum Building in Trinity College (above) was designed by the most famous architects of the time, Sir Thomas Deane and Benjamin Woodward in the Venetian-Byzantine style but using a wide selection of Irish marbles.

A further legacy from the 19th century is Dublin Zoo, one of the oldest such institutions in the world, founded in 1831. As well as a wide variety of animals, its grounds hold this charming lodge (opposite).

That melancholy did not lift even after the greater part of Ireland achieved political independence in the 1920s. The Northern Irish poet Louis MacNeice would write of how Dublin 'holds my mind / With her seedy elegance'. Similarly, visiting the city in the mid-1940s, the English architectural historian James Lees-Milne noted in his diary that 'the squalor of the slums is formidable.... Splendid mid-Georgian grand houses, now tenements in neglect, dirt and disrepair.' For a long time the new state was impoverished, scarcely able to support its inhabitants and certainly not in a position to glorify its capital.

What cannot also be overlooked is the fact that the Irish have always been more an oral than a visual race and therefore the long, sad decline of Dublin was simply not noticed by the majority of its citizens. Nothing better illustrates this circumstance than the want of attention for so long paid to the Liffey which for some two miles flows through the centre of the city. 'No city neglects its river as Dublin does,' declared Oliver St John Gogarty, the inspiration for the character of Buck Mulligan in Joyce's *Ulysses*. Actually, Gogarty was inaccurate because the neglect of the waterway is commonplace in towns and cities throughout Ireland and offers further regrettable proof that the local population is not overly concerned with matters aesthetic.

For much of the past century, even those aware of what was happening were usually untroubled by the dereliction and neglect. Aside from non-national commentators such as Lees-Milne, it was left to a small band of dedicated admirers of architecture and design, most notably the Hon. Desmond Guinness and his late wife Mariga who founded the Irish Georgian Society, to bring the merits of Dublin's heritage to the attention of a wider audience.

Buildings in Dublin were often used to mark important points in the city. At the point where Westmoreland and D'Olier Streets meet O'Connell Bridge and the River Liffey stands this late-19th-century neo-Gothic structure (left) while the top of O'Connell Street concludes with the Assembly Rooms of the Rotunda Hospital, built in 1764 (right).

However, the architectural riches of Dublin, like the fine mansions found throughout the Irish countryside, were too closely associated with the old regime to find much favour in independent Ireland. Many of the city's Georgian buildings became so seriously dilapidated that eventually they had to be abandoned or even demolished. Poor planning on the part of the authorities charged with managing the city made matters worse. By the early 1980s, the singer Bob Geldof, a native of Dublin, could rail against 'the destruction of the city itself, which was once one of the prettiest cities in these islands and is now a shambolic mess, at best.' Dublin's suburbs became increasingly more desirable than the centre as a place to live and gradually the core of the capital was almost abandoned by its citizens. That situation only began to change in the past twenty years, as the merits of urban living were once more appreciated and people chose to move back into the heart of Dublin. Finally, after generations had fled the centre, their descendants began to return there.

In their wake came new shops, pubs, restaurants and hotels; thankfully, the revival of city-centre living has proved to be less transitory than many of these facilities. For a period in the 1990s, Dublin became intensely fashionable among international travellers. Magazines described it as the 'hippest' city in Europe and enthused over its bars and nightclubs. It became a favourite weekend choice for English stag and hen parties which flooded into the revitalized Temple Bar area of the city. For Dubliners who had made the decision to move into the old centre of the capital, fashionability was a mixed blessing of which publicans appeared to be the principal beneficiaries. To live in the midst of a tourist resort was no more pleasant than to remain in a melancholic and semi-ruinous city.

For more than two centuries, one of the most familiar sights of the city's skyline has been the limestone drum and copper dome of the Four Courts, built during the last decades of the 18th century to the designs of James Gandon. The building was gutted by fire during the Civil War of 1922 but afterwards entirely reconstructed.

To live in Dublin is to have the surrounding countryside within easy reach. In nearby County Wicklow can be found Powerscourt House and its gardens. The former was destroyed by an accidental fire in 1974 but the grounds remain as spectacular as ever. Their most glorious feature is the sequence of Italianate terraces leading down to the Triton Pool with its fountain jets, offering romantic views across the landscape to the distant Sugarloaf Mountain.

For much of the past century, therefore, living in Dublin has not been either easy or even necessarily desirable. And to live in the city now is still somewhat to participate in a sociological experiment. Even today, the Irish frequently remain unfamiliar with the finer nuances of urban life and this gives the city a gritty character so well conveyed in the novels of Roddy Doyle such as *The Commitments* and *The Snapper*. Dublin lacks the refinements of cities such as Paris or Rome and visitors seeking urbanity among the native population are likely to be disappointed. Dublin is closer in spirit to Naples or Barcelona; living there can be rough at times because all social groups and classes are mingled together. Just behind Merrion Square, one of the city's finest examples of 18th-century urban design, lie large blocks of cheap local authority housing, thus ensuring that the richest and poorest residents of Dublin are constantly meeting each other.

Is this necessarily a drawback? If Dublin has changed in the recent past, one enduring characteristic is its sociability. It is almost impossible for any Dubliner to walk through the main thoroughfares without meeting

Water, water everywhere. Whether the sea which wraps itself around the coastline of Dublin (left) or the inland lakes found in abundance in County Wicklow to the immediate south. And, of course, both are regularly replenished by Ireland's abundant rainfall.

Dublin does not enjoy an especially temperate climate. Despite this, many of the city's residents like to swim in the sea and one of the most famous places for doing so is at the Forty Foot in Sandycove. Its name derives from the English army's Fortieth Foot regiment which was stationed in the nearby tower during the 19th century. The Forty Foot used to be famous as a place where only men were permitted to bathe and nudity was the norm. Periodically, groups of women would invade the site and proclaim their right to swim there also. Now they do so all the time and a sign announces that 'togs must be worn' (although clusters of resolutely naked men can still be spotted lurking among the rocks).

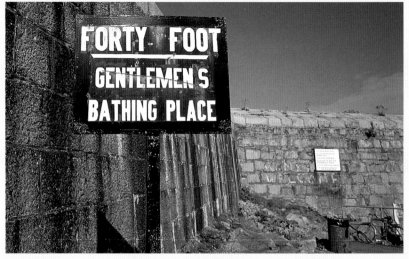

One of the glories of Dublin is its bay, a great hemisphere running from Howth Head in the north to Killiney Head in the south; on a clear day (not necessarily a frequent occurrence), it is possible to see one from the other. This is the first sight of Dublin for visitors arriving by boat and the last for those leaving in the same way. For the athletically inclined, almost the entire distance can be covered on foot, particularly when the tide is out and Dubliners flock to take exercise on the shores of their bay. Pretty 19th-century villages — now all part of the capital's suburbs — cover land along the way. An alternative means to explore the bay is provided by the light railway line known as the DART which runs its lengths from north to south with regular stops en route.

at least one acquaintance. The compact core of the capital, running from St Stephen's Green to Parnell Square remains one of the most intensely social places in Europe. Dubliners are notoriously talkative; like all members of the Irish race, they love language and, even more importantly, they relish an opportunity to demonstrate their ability to play with it. Conversation in Ireland is an artform, and the national skill is amply demonstrated by Dubliners, not least in their fondness for giving nicknames to public monuments. So a statue showing the 18th-century barrow girl Molly Malone on Grafton Street has been dubbed the 'tart with the cart', due to the impressive décolletage of her dress, while a fountain which used to be on O'Connell Street and was intended to depict the Liffey in the character of Anna Livia came to be known as the 'floozie in the jacuzzi'.

The increasing numbers of tourists visiting Dublin certainly do not come to the city to enjoy its climate, and not necessarily for its architecture or other cultural opportunities. Primarily, Dublin retains an allure because of its citizens and it is for the same reason that living there continues to be an attractive proposition. The city's traffic is invariably congested and often anarchic, its streets overcrowded and scruffy – after all, the traditional epithet of 'dirty Dublin' was not bestowed without good reason – its services both public and private operating seemingly without any order. And yet locals love the place. The explanation for Dublin's perverse appeal lies in her people, their loquaciousness, their friendliness, their ability to charm not just visitors but each other. Other aspects of Dublin may be subject to constant alteration but her speech remains the same. Were James Joyce somehow to return to the city he commemorated in *Ulysses*, he might not recognize many of the buildings and streets, but he would undoubtedly still be familiar with the language of the locals.

The largest southern coastal suburb of Dublin is Dun Laoghaire (left), once an insignificant fishing village which became an important town soon after the construction of its port from 1815 onwards. Today, Dun Laoghaire runs without break into the adjacent village of Sandycove (overleaf).

GEORGIAN

If Dublin ever experienced a golden age, it was during the 18th century, when prosperity and a large degree of independence saw the city become one of the most beautiful capitals in Europe. A long period of decline would follow, during which much of Dublin's Georgian architecture fell into ruin, but of late the importance of this heritage has become better appreciated and previously neglected buildings have been rescued from decay and restored.

An 18th-century city residence in the early morning light.

O ver the course of a century, from around 1700 onwards, Dublin underwent a metamorphosis which saw it change from a war-ravaged and impoverished provincial town into a European capital replete with superb examples of classical architecture. The confidence of the citizens during this period was such that they were prepared to pull down almost all evidence of Dublin's past and rebuild entire districts. The majority of the city's major public buildings today date from the 18th century, as does a wealth of private mansions built on splendid squares and streets.

Work began on the redevelopment of Dublin even before 1700; during the previous 100 years, its medieval fabric had been irreparably damaged by successive assaults from rival armies and the consequent

Lined with houses, churches and public buildings, the quays of Dublin (left) were first constructed during the 18th century. The same period saw the beginning of the city's development beyond its medieval walls into areas such as Rathmines (above).

impoverishment of its populace. When James Butler, first Duke of Ormonde, arrived in the city in 1662 to serve as the British government's viceroy, he found Dublin in such poor condition that almost entire reconstruction was considered necessary.

Few of Ormonde's civic enterprises now survive other than his creation of the Phoenix Park on the north-west banks of the River Liffey. Running to over 1,750 acres – twice the size of New York's Central Park – and with a circumference of seven miles, this public amenity lies close to the centre of the city and continues to be much appreciated by Dubliners. Its curious name derives from the anglicization of the Gaelic term *Fionn uisce* meaning 'clear water', a reference to one of the springs found within the park. Nevertheless, at its very centre can be seen a phoenix surmounting a Corinthian column; this was erected in 1747 by one of Ormonde's viceregal successors, the Earl of Chesterfield, who carried out a number of improvements in the area.

Lord Chesterfield also concerned himself with improving the appearance of Dublin Castle, a conglomeration of structures dating back to the reign of King John in the early 13th century. Like so much of the city, it now retains little of its medieval appearance, having suffered from alternating periods of neglect and assault. The present layout of two large quadrangular courtyards was designed by the Surveyor-General, Sir William Robinson, in the late 17th century, but the buildings seen today are predominantly of an even later date. Chesterfield's main contribution was the construction of St Patrick's Hall, where the assemblies, levees and balls, which were such a feature of viceregal social life, were held.

The classical style of architecture flourished gloriously during the Georgian era and for a long time afterwards. Among its glories in Dublin were the Marino Casino (top) built for the Earl of Charlemont in 1762 and the Four Courts (far right) in the centre of Dublin, begun just over twenty years later. Their abiding influence can be seen in the façade of the mid-Victorian Natural History Museum (right).

One of Dublin's best-loved
monuments from the Georgian era,
the Ha'penny Bridge (above).
Its name derives from the half-penny
toll charged to pedestrians after the
bridge was first erected over the Liffey
in 1816. The structure used to be
covered in advertising hoardings and
was allowed to fall into neglect; it has
recently been restored to its original
splendour and has been joined by
a neighbouring pedestrian bridge.
Almost one hundred years earlier,

Dublin's first public hospital opened
thanks to a bequest from Dr Richard
Steevens who died in 1710 (right).
Its enchanting courtyard was designed
by Thomas Burgh, also responsible for
the library at Trinity College and for
the Collins Army Barracks, which
almost faces the hospital across the
Liffey. Dr Steevens' foundation no
longer serves its original purpose, but
acts as headquarters for the local health
authority which was responsible for
the restoration of the building.

The philanthropic concerns of the Georgian age led to the construction of some wonderful buildings in Dublin, including Europe's first maternity hospital, the Rotunda (right) founded by Dr Mosse in 1750; its chapel (above) contains wonderful plasterwork. Even earlier in date is the Royal Hospital Kilmainham (overleaf) dating from the 1680s and now the Irish Museum of Modern Art.

The same spirit of welcome today pervades another Georgian building originally associated with the ruling British regime. Close by Lord Chesterfield's monument in the Phoenix Park stands Aras an Uachtarain, built in 1751 by the Irish gentleman-architect Nathaniel Clements. Formerly the viceregal lodge and it is now the official residence of the President of Ireland.

To return to the man responsible for creating that park, the first Duke of Ormonde, there is one other abiding monument to his period as viceroy in Ireland, the Royal Hospital Kilmainham. Built between 1671 and 1676 on rising ground across the river from the Phoenix Park, it was designed by Sir William Robinson and intended to serve the same purpose as Les Invalides in Paris: a retirement home for some three hundred elderly soldiers. The last military pensioner left the Royal Hospital in 1927 and the building suffered a long period of neglect. However, since the early 1990s, the entire site has served as the Irish Museum of Modern Art.

Perhaps the greatest example of Georgian philanthropy is a complex of buildings known as the Rotunda which opened its doors in 1745 as the first maternity hospital in Europe, a function it still continues to perform. The chapel, decorated by the stuccoer Barthelemy Cramillion, is especially worth seeing, a ravishing example of rococo ornamentation with an abundance of cherubs romping across its ceiling. The Rotunda was established by Bartholomew Mosse, a polymath whose principal career was medicine but who also found time to act as a brilliant entrepreneur. The circular assembly room which gave the Rotunda its name was added in 1764, five years after Dr Mosse's early death.

Behind the hospital stands one of the finest of the private residences built by Dublin's Georgian grandees. This is Charlemont House, designed by Sir William Chambers for the Earl of Charlemont. Today it is the Municipal Art Gallery, housing a collection of Barbizon and Impressionist pictures donated to Dublin by a later philanthropist, Sir Hugh Lane. The gallery lies at the centre of Parnell Square, once called Rutland Square, and probably the most prestigious address in

the city. In the 1790s it was home to eleven peers, two bishops and twelve Members of Parliament.

Indeed, for much of the 18th century, it was the northside of Dublin that attracted the affluent, unlike the present time when those with money as a rule prefer to live south of the Liffey. It was on the latter side of the river that the original city settlement had taken place, so when new areas were being developed during the decades of peace from 1690 onwards, there was a natural inclination to look northwards to virgin land.

Much of this development was undertaken by the Gardiners, a family of property speculators who were eventually ennobled as Earls of Blessington. They created what was, in effect, a new city, with wide boulevards and large private residences. Changes in taste have meant that not all this streetscape still survives, but evidence of their ambitions can be found in Mountjoy Square and Henrietta Street, the latter lined with the biggest houses built in the city, including the Gardiners' own home. Then there is North Great George's Street which terminates in Belvedere House, another palatial residence built for one of Georgian Dublin's wealthiest residents. A Jesuit school since 1841 — James Joyce was a pupil here for a relatively brief period and its lasting influence on him can be found in his *Portrait of the Artist as a Young Man* — Belvedere House has the most perfect series of neoclassical interiors in Dublin, with several rooms named after classical gods whose exploits they celebrate in stucco decoration.

A house in Rathmines (left). The Georgian doorways of Dublin: as idiosyncratic as the people who live behind them (above).

GEORGIAN
RENOVATION

Restoring an old house in Dublin seems to take almost as long as its original building. This 18th-century residence of the distinguished Irish couturier Jen Kelly, has been undergoing renovation for over a decade and the work is only now nearing completion. Although a previous owner had finished all essential refurbishment, Kelly says when he first visited the house, 'it was so cold that I had to go to bed for three days afterwards.'

Like many other houses in this area of Dublin, the one now owned by Jen Kelly had fallen into decline within a century of being built. Standing close to the top of North Great George's Street, the property appears to date from the first half of the 18th century, before this part of the city was formally laid out. While initially a fashionable address, more and more poor people gradually moved into the area until this particular house was home to twenty-six different families, all of them sharing a single bathroom. They had moved out before Kelly moved in, but the visible effects of the house's long decline can still be seen throughout its interior, not least on walls stripped of all decoration, exposing their original Georgian brickwork.

Originally from Northern Ireland, but resident in Dublin for a couple of decades, Jen Kelly used to live and run his business in different parts of the city. Now they are combined under the same roof and in magnificent surroundings. Kelly believes that the house was first erected for a Church of Ireland bishop, because all such clergymen would have owned princely residences in Ireland's Georgian capital and spent much of their time there. Of particular interest is the plasterwork in some rooms, which contains symbols and tools associated with Freemasonry. According to Kelly, the house could therefore have acted as a masonic lodge especially as clerics were often connected with this movement during the 18th century. Nevertheless, he says, 'it's certainly very spiritual here. I've never felt lonely and I think the house must hold very happy memories.'

Despite the grand size of its rooms, Jen Kelly's house is warm and even cosy. Its owner likes to dine by candlelight in the winter evenings and makes a point of using every part of the house, even though its three principal reception rooms still await full redecoration. With his business in the basement — 'that's the engine to the whole house,' he remarks — and his bedroom on the top floor, Mr Kelly gets plenty of exercise, regularly running up and down the property's five storeys accompanied by his two dogs, a Siberian Husky and an Old English Sheepdog.

Among the house's distinctive features is a mixture of different 18th-century styles, from rococo to neoclassical. Jen Kelly believes that one of the rooms may have been decorated by the Dublin stuccoer Robert West, whose own extravagantly ornamented former house on Dominick Street still stands. Somehow, much of the original plasterwork survived the many years of neglect and decay until rescued and restored by a sympathetic owner. 'I love living in this part of the city,' comments Kelly. 'The northside of Dublin has had a lot of taboos, but I think we're dispelling those.'

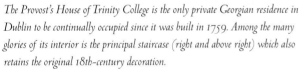

The Provost's House of Trinity College is the only private Georgian residence in Dublin to be continually occupied since it was built in 1759. Among the many glories of its interior is the principal staircase (right and above right) which also retains the original 18th-century decoration.

A decade later in date is City Hall, an abiding tribute to the prosperity of Dublin's Georgian merchants for whom it was constructed as an exchange (far right and above left). The first neoclassical building in the city, it was designed by Thomas Cooley, who died young in 1784. When the capital's economy declined in the 19th century, City Hall was acquired by Dublin's governing body, which has recently restored the property to the appearance it had over two hundred years ago.

Walking through this part of Dublin now, the abiding impression received is of grandeur either faded or lost altogether. There have been many reasons given why the northern inner city should have failed to retain its fashionable status. One of the most frequently cited is the decision by the first Duke of Leinster to locate his own immense townhouse south of the Liffey. When work began in 1745, the Duke was advised that the site chosen for the building stood far from the period's centre of taste and he supposedly retorted that society would follow wherever he went. Clad in grey limestone, Leinster House has a sombre appearance, but the interiors are elegant, if somewhat austere, and they now provide accommodation for the Dáil, the Irish parliament, which has been based here since 1922.

Merrion and Fitzwilliam Squares, begun in 1762 and 1791 respectively, demonstrate that the Duke of Leinster's prediction about society following his lead was correct. Probably the finest of Dublin's Georgian squares – until badly mauled by property developers during the second half of the 20th century – was St Stephen's Green, first marked out for residential use in 1664, but not put to that purpose until some time later. The central square, long accessible only to householders who possessed a key to the gates, was bought in 1877 by Lord Ardilaun, a member of the Guinness family, who then paid for the park to be landscaped before presenting it to the citizens of Dublin. While a large number of the 18th-century houses around St Stephen's Green have been demolished, some splendid buildings do remain. Along the northside of the square is the Shelbourne Hotel which opened in 1824, the oldest and most famous such hostelry in Dublin. On the opposite side of St Stephen's Green stand more magnificent old mansions, among them Iveagh House which, thanks to another act of Guinness generosity, today serves as the Irish Department of Foreign Affairs.

The 18th-century State Apartments of Dublin Castle were used for receptions and balls during the years of British rule in Ireland. In the 1780s, the Earl of Caernarvon's sister wrote that she went to parties in the castle at least twice a week.

A suite of ornate rooms in Dublin
Castle leads to the Throne Room where
the Lord Lieutenant, representing the
British monarch, would sit and welcome
his guests to the building (above).
For centuries, this is where young
Irish debutantes would be received
into Dublin society for the first time.
At the other end of Dame Street,
equally splendid receptions were held in
the first-floor salon of the Provost's
House at Trinity College (right).
A copy of one of Lord Burlington's
Palladian designs, its first occupant
was the bachelor Francis Andrews.
At the end of the salon hangs a
portrait of his friend and patron the
Duke of Bedford, painted by
Thomas Gainsborough.

GEORGIAN
GRANDEUR

Ormonde Quay was the first riverside district of Dublin to be developed for residential use; as its name implies, building there took place during the period that the first Duke of Ormonde was viceroy for the British crown in the 17th century. The house illustrated here dates from 1745. Among its most striking features is a top-lit stairwell running up the centre of the house.

The Ormonde Quay residence was built for another aristocrat, the first Earl of Belvedere, whose son would move into an even grander property, Belvedere House, which now closes North Great George's Street. The quayside house had been leased to one of the period's most successful bankers, John La Touche, who may have run his business from the premises, as a bank vault still survives in the basement. Unlike so many other Georgian houses in central Dublin, this one never became divided into tenements, but by the 19th century it was used as offices and later came to serve as a tie factory; a large extension for this purpose was added over what had been the back garden. By the time the present owner's predecessor bought the building, it was in a semi-ruinous condition, the roof so badly decayed that the fourth floor had collapsed into the third.

Despite its considerable size – each floor runs to some 1,400 square feet – the building feels extremely comfortable and warm. As the restoration of the such houses continues, living in Georgian Dublin looks like having a long future.

Having lived in London for a number of years, in the late 1990s, John Lynch decided to move back to his native country; 'I recognised the value of Georgian properties. This house totally grabbed me as soon as I saw it.'

Each of the five floors in John Lynch's quayside home runs to around 1,400 square feet. On the two upper levels, he has a number of bedrooms and living areas as well as a roof terrace where he spends most of his own time. 'It's like living in a relatively small house on top of a much bigger one,' he smiles, 'but I always have the advantage of using both if I want.'

The principal reception rooms are decorated in a style and on a scale that suit their grand proportions with an abundance of gilt mirrors and fine objets d'art.

During the extended period of peace and prosperity in the 18th century, Ireland's capital played host to the country's parliament, housed in superb purpose-built premises on College Green. Designed by the Palladian architect Sir Edward Lovett Pearce and erected between 1729 and 1739, they were later extended by James Gandon to provide a separate entrance for the House of Lords. The latter chamber remains unaltered and can be visited, but the rest of the building was extensively refurbished by the Bank of Ireland after the country's parliament was abolished by the British government following the Act of Union of 1800. Some twenty-one years before that date, it was described by an overseas visitor as 'one of the most perfect pieces of architecture in Europe.'

The former parliament offers eloquent testimony to the confidence of 18th-century Dublin, and so too does its neighbour Trinity College which was given its present appearance during much the same period, although it had been in fact founded by Queen Elizabeth I in 1592. The earliest extant structure within its walls is a red-brick range of accommodation dating from 1700 called the Rubrics. At a right-angle to this is one of the college's greatest glories, the old library designed in 1712 by Thomas Burgh; its ground floor was once an open arcade, until demand for more space in the late 19th century required that this be closed. Above stands the barrel-vaulted Long Room, which at a length of 209 feet amply justifies its name. The other key 18th-century buildings in the college complex are the Chapel and Examination Hall, both designed in the 1770s by Sir William Chambers and facing one another across Front Square, Richard Castle's Dining Hall some thirty years earlier in date and the principal Palladian façade of 1752 looking up Dame Street towards Dublin Castle.

The abiding influence of the Georgian age. Now Government Buildings, but originally built for University College Dublin, this building (left) dates from the early 20th century. The façade right, on the other hand, is authentic; it was designed in 1773 to house the Blue Coat School, established a century earlier by King Charles II.

Trinity College and the Houses of Parliament are just two of the substantial public buildings erected in the city during the Georgian age, but there are many others of equal splendour and importance, not least the Custom House which was first responsible for bringing the English architect James Gandon to Ireland in 1781. Dublin's importance as a port is shown by the scale of this work – 375 feet long – and by its elaborate decoration. Carved busts representing Ireland's fourteen most important rivers running along the waterside portico. The same architect also took on the task of designing the Four Courts for the hearing of legal cases. Overlooking the river west of the Custom House, the Four Courts is capped by an enormous copper dome which stands out on the city skyline at sunset. Both buildings were gutted by fire during the troubles accompanying Ireland's struggle for independence and as a result their original interiors – and contents – were destroyed. In the case of the Four Courts, this was a very serious loss; the premises had held the Public Records Office, with historical documents dating back to the 12th century.

Copper-covered domes are found throughout Dublin, such as those capping James Gandon's Custom House of 1789 (left) and the Church of St Stephen's, which closes Upper Mount Street (above). The unusual line of the latter's roofline has led to it being popularly known as the Peppercannister Church.

This vast archive disappeared in a fire which blazed for five days before it was brought under control. In those flames perished an enormous amount of information about Georgian Dublin, forever limiting the extent of our knowledge about that glorious period.

James Gandon accepted the task of designing the Four Courts following the death in 1784 of another architect, Thomas Cooley, who had drawn up plans for the site. But Cooley left one masterpiece completed before his death, City Hall, which closes Parliament Street and can be seen from far down Capel Street on the opposite side of the river. The hall was built as a new exchange for Dublin's merchants, sufficiently rich in the 1770s to afford palatial premises in the neoclassical style, with Portland stone used for exterior and interior alike. The decline of mercantile business during the 19th century meant that the building was sold in 1852 to Dublin Corporation which adapted it for use as civic offices. In the late 1990s the entire premises were restored by the city authorities to Cooley's first designs and opened to the public.

Facing City Hall is yet more proof of the wealth of Georgian Dublin: the former Newcomen Bank of 1781. Just one of many private financial institutions which thrived (and occasionally failed) in the 18th century, it was designed by Thomas Ivory, who was also the architect of the old Blue Coat School built in 1773 on Blackhall Place. Banks in the 18th century were private concerns, usually owned by families such as the La Touches, originally Huguenots from France who grew so wealthy from their enterprise that they owned townhouses in both St Stephen's Green and Merrion Square.

The La Touches were also enlightened patrons of the arts and sciences, but the benefits of this are now perhaps less evident than those of the Wide Street Commissioners. Created by an Act of Parliament in 1757, the purpose of this organization is evident in its name. Particularly on the southside of the Liffey, the Commissioners were responsible for giving the main routes across central Dublin the form they continue to have today. Perhaps the body's single most important

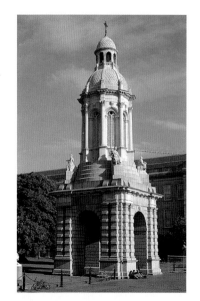

A century separates the Campanile of Trinity College (above) from the tower rising over the entrance to Dublin Castle (right), but they share the same spirit and grace. The campanile is located on what was believed to be the site of the belltower of the Augustinian monastery which occupied this part of Dublin, prior to the establishment of the college in 1592.

act was the decision taken in 1782 to build a new bridge across the Liffey linking the fashionable districts of the north with those just beginning to be developed on the other side of the river. O'Connell Bridge, as it is now called, draws traffic from Trinity College and the Bank of Ireland along Westmoreland and D'Olier Streets (both of them laid out under the direction of the Commissioners) and over to Dublin's principal thoroughfare, O'Connell Street – another route that originated in the mid-18th century when it was first known as Gardiner's Mall.

The Wide Street Commissioners continued in existence until 1841 – but long before then their powers had begun to deteriorate, as had the prestige and glory of Georgian Dublin. No one has ever produced an entirely satisfactory explanation for the city's extended period of decline, from the early 19th until the late 20th century. However, it is clear that the loss of a semi-autonomous parliament following the Act of Union in 1800 had a negative effect on Ireland's capital. From that date until independence was achieved in the 1920s, anyone who wished to have an influence on the country's development was obliged to go to London, where all all Irish-related legislation was debated and passed in the British Houses of Parliament.

The impact on Dublin's social, economic and cultural life was quickly felt. Before the Act of Union, almost 250 peers and 300 members of the Irish House of Commons had lived in the city; just over twenty years later, those figures had dropped to thirty-four peers and five members of the British House of Commons. In her novel, *The Absentee*, published in 1812, the Irish novelist Maria Edgeworth complained about 'the want of manners, joined to the want of knowledge' now found in Dublin. But there was also a want of money in the capital, and that remained the case for much of the next two centuries. Without money there could be no fresh development, just impoverishment or, at best, stagnation. Only over the past few decades has affluence returned, and Dubliners have been able once more to attempt the improvement of their native city.

GEORGIAN
ORNAMENT

Extraordinary as it now seems, for almost two hundred years the magnificent Georgian houses of north Dublin were so out of fashion that only the poorest sections of society were prepared to live in them. Whole streets fell into such decay that eventually they either collapsed or were demolished, then cleared away to make room for more hygienic housing. Therefore, while a lot of 18th-century Dublin's character remains, just as much of it has gone forever.

More still might have disappeared but for the enterprising character of a few pioneers who, long before this part of the city began to regain its popularity, were foolhardy enough to move there and begin the arduous process of refurbishment and regeneration. Among the first of this brave group was Desiree Shortt who bought her home on North Great George's Street in 1975. At that time, the house had twenty-seven sitting tenants, the last of whom only left eighteen years later, thereby permitting access to the superb first-floor drawing-room.

The house dates from 1785 when it was built by the stuccoer Charles Thorpe, presumably as his own residence but also as a showcase for his talents; Thorpe would later go on to become Lord Mayor of Dublin, so clearly he enjoyed a prosperous career. Examples of his work can still be seen in the building, in particular on the ceilings of the two first-floor reception rooms. These probably survived almost intact because of the

Examples of Charles Thorpe's plasterwork can still be seen throughout the building. His refined neoclassicism is in marked contrast to the exuberant rococo style which remained fashionable in Dublin until the last decades of the 18th century.

rooms' height; none of the seventeen layers of wallpaper which had to be removed to get back to the original paintwork reached as high as Charles Thorpe's delicate neoclassical plasterwork. So while this had to be cleaned to remove the dense accretions of smoke and grime acquired while the house had been divided into tenements, it was otherwise in fine condition.

This particular building had not suffered from too many generations of abuse. At some point in the 19th century, it was acquired by the establishment Church of Ireland which, in turn, rented out the house in the 1870s to a remarkable academic called Sir John Pentland Mahaffy. He and his family lived there until 1914 when they moved to the still grander surroundings of the Provost's House in Trinity College, following his appointment to that institution's highest office. The period of decline for this home only started after the Irish Civil War in the early 1920s, when the general poverty of the city and country meant few people could afford the number of servants needed to support such a house.

Before its restoration to past splendours, the house's twenty-seven tenants washed, slept and cooked in their own rented spaces, sharing the building's one bathroom which was suspended from the back of the second floor. Having nowhere else to go, the present owner lived in a backroom in the basement for the first seventeen years of ownership, but has now reclaimed the whole house. More houses in the area have been restored and occupied, bringing the tenement era to a close and ensuring that Dublin's Georgian architecture is once more appreciated.

Decorated in Georgian style throughout, no evidence remains of the degradation suffered by this house during the last century. Among its principal charms are the delightful roundels which were part of the original decoration designed by the building's first owner, Charles Thorpe.

Having nowhere else to go, the present owner lived in a backroom in the basement for seventeen years after the house was bought in 1975. Today, as the building's single occupant, she can afford to give herself a generous amount of accommodation, including this fine bedroom with its carved fireplace on the second floor. Prior to retiring in 2000, she also ran a successful china-restoration business from the property. Since moving into the area, she has seen it undergo many changes as more and more houses are restored and occupied, often by individuals or even families with children.

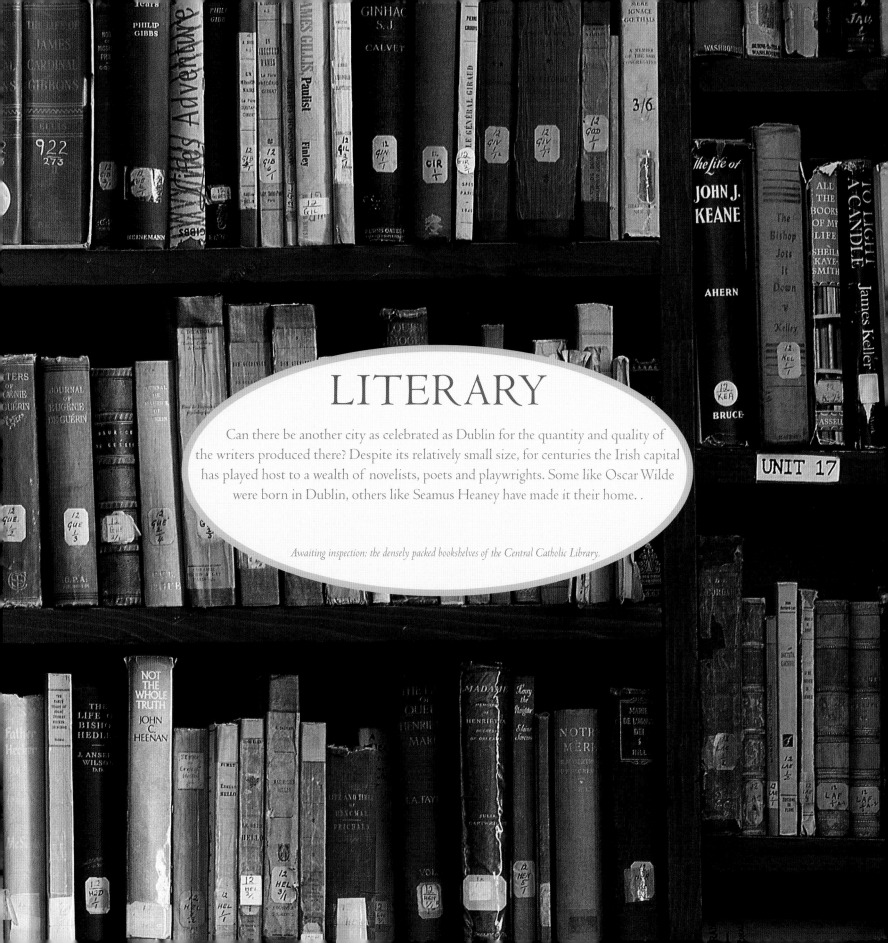

LITERARY

Can there be another city as celebrated as Dublin for the quantity and quality of the writers produced there? Despite its relatively small size, for centuries the Irish capital has played host to a wealth of novelists, poets and playwrights. Some like Oscar Wilde were born in Dublin, others like Seamus Heaney have made it their home. .

Awaiting inspection: the densely packed bookshelves of the Central Catholic Library.

D ublin's literary reputation has a more recent lineage than might initially appear to be the case. Ancient Gaelic myths and sagas were primarily recited by bards and only rarely written down. Furthermore, almost until the 18th century, Dublin's relatively small population was scarcely large enough to sustain many writers. The peace experienced by Georgian Ireland, the prosperity of that period and the presence in the centre of the capital of Trinity College all helped to create circumstances in which a literary culture could develop. The college's undergraduates were not always the most studious and were renowned as much for their rowdiness as for their academic prowess. Even so, they created a demand for new writing and a large number of Irish authors from this period were graduates of Trinity College.

But perhaps the students and their lecturers could not provide a sufficient market. 'Dublin is the poorest place in the world for subscriptions to books,' declared the city's best-known publisher, George Faulkner, in 1758, adding, 'It is much easier to get a hundred dinners, with as many dozen bottles of claret, than a single guinea for the best author.'

Price's Medical Hall on Clare Street (above) is one of the premises mentioned by James Joyce in Ulysses *and the writer would also have been familiar with the nearby bookshop of Greene & Co., which has occupied the same site since the 19th century. Not far away stands 1 Merrion Square, (overleaf) the childhood home of Oscar Wilde. Across Dublin, plaques acknowledge the city's authors, all of them commemorated in the Dublin Writers' Museum on Parnell Square.*

LITERARY
FLAIR

Dublin today is home to as many writers as was ever the case, some of them born in the city, others drawn to it from elsewhere in Ireland or abroad. All of them find a warm welcome there, as well as the potential threat of many distractions. The wise writer will take advantage of the opportunities provided by Dublin, not least the chance to benefit from the proximity of other members of the same profession, without succumbing to the city's attractions.

Why for hundreds of years has Dublin proved to be the crucible in which so many writers of genius were formed? Why is it that four writers either born or resident in Dublin have won the Nobel Prize for Literature: George Bernard Shaw; James Joyce; Samuel Beckett; and Seamus Heaney? Perhaps an explanation lies in the fact that two languages, English and Gaelic, have had to co-exist in the city and that each has fertilized the other. Certainly, the way in which the former tongue is spoken and written in Ireland can be very different – and often much richer – than in England because it has benefited from a secondary influence.

The presence of the Gaelic language in Irish writing is ubiquitous but rarely overt. Nevertheless, its mark can be seen in such seemingly diverse writers as Samuel Beckett and George Bernard Shaw. After all, Gaelic was spoken throughout Ireland until its use began to be actively discouraged by English governments in the 16th and 17th centuries. Its presence can still be felt in the distinctive Hiberno-English spoken in Dublin and elsewhere around the country. The construction of certain commonly employed sentences, such as those beginning, 'I do be...' or 'I'm after doing/going/saying...', are a direct translation from the Gaelic, as is the use of adjectives as adverbs, a typical instance being,

When Irish writer Colm Toibin bought his present home in 1997, it was used as offices and contained, he says, 'terrible carpets and curtains and light fittings'. The narrow Georgian house close to Fitzwilliam Square was, he believes, built as an infill after its neighbours had been completed. Toibin has lived in many other houses in this part of central Dublin since moving to the city from his native Enniscorthy in County Wexford in the early 1970s. 'If you're from a provincial town,' he explains, 'coming to the capital seems to be the most natural thing; I can't even say I liked it when I first came there.'

With his friend, interior designer Lizzie Van Anerongen, Colm Toibin undertook a complete overhaul of the house which had lost all of its original fireplaces as well as many other old fittings. 'It's really not my skill,' he says, 'but I'd seen what Lizzie had done for someone else and then she told me that she could only make cosy and warm spaces so I just let her loose. I don't think I ever said I didn't like anything she did.'

Toibin's bedroom (above) is typical of the house's present character. The paintings here are by Irish artist Mary Lohan; all the art in this room shares the theme of water. On the floor are an orderly line of espadrilles from Barcelona which Toibin regularly visits. 'Everytime I go anywhere, I bring something back, however small. The espadrilles are for decoration, I like to look at them there in the morning.'

At the heart of Colm Toibin's house is his second-floor bookroom. 'I think you need to have a bigger room before you can call it a library,' he insists. The space is entirely self-contained, 'like a cave or a hidden room,' says Toibin who often lights a fire here before spending the day at work.

The writer, whose novel The Blackwater Lightship was shortlisted for the Booker Prize in 1999, has yet to feature Dublin in any of his fiction. 'I've never put the city into a novel. I can only write about places I regret having left or lost such as Enniscorthy and the Wexford coastline or Barcelona or Buenos Aires. What I'm doing with Dublin is building up to a big book when I've left it. It's there to be lost.' Toibin quotes the poet Elizabeth Bishop that the art of losing is not hard to master but the likelihood of mislaying his Dublin home seems unlikely.

'The house felt fierce empty', from Dubliner Conor McPherson's play *Port Authority*. The reason for this is that Ireland's traditional language has never recognized the difference between the two modifying forms. Visitors to the city will also notice a preference among its residents for strong rather than mild descriptive terms – 'You're a shocking decent man', perhaps, or 'The weather was only desperate' – which derive from Gaelic speech.

But above all, it has long been the mark of writers resident in Dublin – and indeed of all Dubliners – to revel in the possibilities of language, to explore its potential and challenge its supposed limitations. And the best, if not only, means for the city's visitors to discover for themselves this persistent linguistic jubilation is to walk the same streets and spend time in the same places as the local population. It is a feature of both Gaelic and Hiberno-English that their speakers take pleasure from the sound of words and the rhythms of speech. Commenting on a remark of St Augustine, Samuel Beckett drew attention to its form and not its content when he said, 'That sentence has a wonderful shape. It is the shape that matters.' For many Dubliners, the shape of words has always mattered. The poet Thomas Moore declared that he was far more confident of the sound of his *Irish Melodies* than of their sense.

Generations of writers have left their mark on the language of Dublin and, in turn, been marked by it. The city's most famous celebrator was James Joyce who, although he spent the greater part of his life far from the city, wrote repeatedly of her, especially in *Ulysses* which is really a celebration of his birthplace. The character of Dublin, especially the indomitable nature and wit of her poorest citizens, has been a leitmotif for writers from Sean O'Casey to Roddy Doyle. A variety of 20th-century authors – including Flann O'Brien and Brendan Behan – developed casual Dublin street argot into a seemingly artless literary style. Of late, some of their successors – Neil Jordan, Jim Sheridan – have sought to bring the same linguistic flair to film, as have a new generation of playwrights such as Conor

'I'm told that in this stretch of Dublin there used to be a lot of bedsits,' remarks Colm Toibin who himself lived in just such accommodation nearby for much of the 1970s and 1980s. His own house was never used for this purpose but nevertheless needed a lot of work before it was sufficiently habitable. Among the new spaces created by Toibin and Lizzie Van Anerongen was this ground-floor kitchen (right). The curtains here are made from African embroidered fabric bought in Greenwhich Village, New York, a typical example of the writer's diverse source of furnishings.

McPherson and Mark O'Rowe. Dublin may not make an appearance in their work but her presence can be felt there, sometimes elusive, always pervasive.

Nevertheless, the city has not always cherished her writers and nor have they invariably responded well to her. Poverty and ambition, material need and spiritual hunger are among the reasons why so many Dublin writers, past and present, have felt the need to move elsewhere and thereafter rarely return to the place of their birth. Oscar Wilde, George Bernard Shaw, James Joyce and Samuel Beckett are just the most famous names on such a list, but there have been many more; even today, Irish authors such as Colm McCann and Michael Collins prefer to live far away from their native country. Dublin is not large, she is an intimate city and not all writers respond well to intimacy. They can find Ireland's capital too sociable, too encroaching and insufficiently aloof from their activities. Their departure is understandable, if regrettable.

This is especially the case because Dublin today is almost certainly a more convivial place for writers than ever before. Their material circumstances have improved, thanks to legislation that absolves creative artists from the need to pay income tax. They are, therefore, now able to keep all the money earned from their efforts, although it should be said one aspect of this remains unchanged: it is still too little. The social status of writers has similarly improved. They are no longer the pariahs of former centuries. Many of them now live in the city, if not necessarily in great comfort, then at least with the confidence of greater security than was available to their predecessors. Dublin acts as a draw for the literarily inclined, its reputation as a city that celebrates writing and writers, attracting ever more of the latter. Some of the best-known names among the younger generation of Irish writers now resident in Dublin are Roddy Doyle, Anne Enright, Joseph O'Connor and Keith Ridgway.

These are the keepers of Dublin's literary reputation, but the city is home to many other writers even more famous among the reading public even if their work is

less highly admired by critics. The doyenne of this group is Maeve Binchy, who has lived in the coastal suburb of Dalkey for decades. Her lead in popular fiction has been followed by many other Dublin writers – almost invariably women – such as Marian Keyes and Cathy Kelly, Sheila O'Flanagan and Morag Prunty. Their work offers quite a different view of Dublin from that found in more intentionally serious writing. But it is one most immediately true to a city which, like the writers living there, finds her circumstances in a state of flux and her future – in fact and fiction alike – as yet unclear.

'In Dublin,' Toibin argues, 'you take it for granted that other writers and artists were all over the city. If I want to go to Grafton Street at night, I have the option of walking past where Gerard Manley Hopkins wrote his sonnets on the top floor of Newman House which is where Joyce worked as well. Routes all around the city are redolent with the physical persona of writers like Yeats. It's literary in the sense that the people I used to see in the National Library in the 1970s are still there and I still see them thirty years later.' On the top floor of his Dublin home, the writer has made a refuge in which he can sleep and wash in spacious comfort as one space opens into another (above and left).

One sign of a growing literary culture was the abundance of newspapers produced at the time, precursors of today's healthy Irish media. Those that appeared in the 18th century had names such as *The Dublin Intelligence*, *The Dublin Packet* and *The Dublin Weekly Journal*. Only a small number lasted more than a few years, although one, *The Freeman's Journal* which made its debut in 1763, continued to be published for almost two centuries.

A more enduring presence was the theatre, the first of which opened in Dublin in the 1630s; this was closed a few years later by the Puritan forces of Oliver Cromwell on his expedition to Ireland. Although the Irish wrote little drama of lasting merit during the 17th century, an exception ought to be made for George Farquhar whose most famous plays, *The Beaux' Strategem* and *The Recruiting Officer* are still occasionally performed.

Farquhar began his career as an actor in Dublin, but abandoned this profession after wounding a fellow-player on stage by using a real sword rather than a prop. The venue in which this accident took place was the Smock Alley Theatre, the most celebrated in 18th-century Ireland, if only for the number of disasters

In 1904 James Joyce very briefly lived in an early 19th-century Martello Tower at Sandycove with his friend Oliver St John Gogarty. Today, it is a museum dedicated to the writer who understandably found the conditions here too uncomfortable.

occurring there. For much of the 18th century it was an extremely popular, if potentially riotous, venue. Dublin theatres today are much more placid places, although the Abbey Theatre did witness a number of riots over plays during the first decades of the 20th century.

For some years after 1745, the Smock Alley Theatre was managed by Thomas Sheridan, a close friend of Swift but more familiar today as the father of Richard Brinsley Sheridan. It is a pity that the latter's great plays, *The School for Scandal* and *The Rivals*, like *She Stoops to Conquer* by another Irishman, Oliver Goldsmith, were first performed in London where both writers chose to spend their adult lives. This was a long-standing problem for impresarios in Dublin, which could not compete with the larger audiences – and fees – offered by the English capital. Towards the end of the 18th century, a theatre manager called Frederick Jones complained, 'Dublin no market is for wit / 'Tis common – no one values it – / But we export it; and our parts / Bear highest price in foreign parts.'

Such remained the case until the early 1900s when a group of friends including W.B. Yeats and Lady Gregory, decided to start a new company which would stage plays in Dublin written, directed and acted by and for Irish men and women. And so the Abbey Theatre came into existence, although its first years were troubled by disgruntlement among sections of the Dublin public. They disapproved of the language used by J.M. Synge in *The Playboy of the Western World* and, almost twenty years later, vociferously objected to the presence of a prostitute in Sean O'Casey's *The Plough and the Stars*. It was on the latter occasion that Yeats came onto the stage and demanded, 'Is this going to be a recurring celebration of Irish genius?'

It proved not to be so, in part because for decades thereafter the Abbey Theatre only staged the dullest of plays, predominantly timid comedies set in rural Ireland. The building in which it was housed had once been the city morgue and, as the writer Frank O'Connor mordantly observed, it had been 'fully restored to its original purpose'.

The superb first-floor reception rooms of the Dublin Writers Museum in Parnell Square (far left and left) date from the last decade of the 19th century when the house was owned by George Jameson, a member of the wealthy whiskey distilling family. The museum contains memorabilia and information on many historical Irish literary figures; next door is the Irish Writers Centre where contemporary authors can meet. Meanwhile, on North Great George's Street stands a fine 18th-century house dedicated in its entirety to just one writer: the seemingly ubiquitous James Joyce. In premises first built for the Earl of Kenmare and later a dancing academy, Dublin's most famous literary offspring is recalled and celebrated.

From the late 1920s onwards, another Dublin venue, the Gate Theatre, took on the mantle for staging adventurous new productions under the partnership of Hilton Edwards and Micheal MacLiammoir. Today, it might be said that the Abbey and the Gate compete in healthy rivalry to be considered Dublin's premier theatre, the position of both constantly challenged by a wide variety of younger companies and venues in the city centre and its suburbs.

Not all of Dublin's playwrights have remained in their native city. Oscar Wilde rarely returned to Ireland after he won a scholarship to Oxford in 1874. George Bernard Shaw likewise moved to London two years later. But the latter, who never lost his fond memories of the Irish capital, saw a number of his plays performed there and on his death in 1950 left a third of his estate to the National Gallery, a bequest that proved extremely advantageous after the success of the musical *My Fair Lady*, based on Shaw's play *Pygmalion*. Shaw was born in Synge Street in a house that is now a museum dedicated to his memory.

Still, it would be misleading to give the impression that Dublin has been a city from which all writers usually fled. During the 19th century authors, such as Lady Morgan – whose flamboyant actor-manager father Robert Owenson ran a 'National Theatre' in the capital in the 1780s – settled in Dublin. The first woman to receive a literary pension from the state, Lady Morgan and her husband lived for a number of years on Kildare Street where she hosted a famous literary and political salon. Eventually, though, the Morgans did move to London in the belief that there were greater opportunities in the English capital. The middle decades of the century were, indeed, a fairly bleak period for Ireland and for Dublin; the city's misfortunes are reflected in much of the work produced there at the time. The era's foremost poet, James Clarence Mangan – today best remembered for his verses 'Dark Rosaleen' ('O my Dark Rosaleen / Do not sigh, do not weep!') – led a wretched existence addicted to alcohol and opium before his death from cholera and

Doorway of 7 Eccles Street, home of James Joyce's fictional character Leopold Bloom in Ulysses.

malnutrition in 1849 at the age of forty-six. Mangan's gloom reflected not only his own circumstances but also those of the country, his Roisin Dubh or Dark Rosaleen, then suffering from the devastation of the Great Famine which ravaged it for four years and decimated the population.

The confident and affluent Dublin of today appears to have little in common with the unhappy city that inspired both Mangan and his literary idol, Charles Maturin, a cleric who wrote one of the 19th century's most famous gothic novels, *Melmoth the Wanderer*, first published in 1820, four years before the author's death at the age of forty-four. His neice, Lady Wilde, had, before her marriage, begun publishing patriotic verses and articles under the name Speranza for *The Nation*, a journal published weekly by members of the Young Ireland group until it was suppressed by the British government in 1848. When her son Oscar Wilde went into exile in France after his release from prison in 1897, he adopted the pseudonym Sebastian Melmoth, after his great-uncle's fictional hero.

Could the dark character of Dublin at that time also have inspired the work of two other great 19th-century gothic novelists? Joseph Sheridan Le Fanu was the great-nephew of Richard Brinsley Sheridan and lived for much of his life at 70 Merrion Square, now the headquarters of Ireland's Arts Council. Following his wife's early death, he became a virtual recluse, taking to his bed where, between midnight and dawn, to avoid the nightmares that haunted his sleep, he wrote ghost stories. These included *Carmilla*, the tale of a beautiful young vampire who likes to make potential victims fall in love with her before killing them. This story anticipates the more famous such work *Dracula* by another Dublin-born writer, Bram Stoker.

One common response from Dublin writers when faced with survival in a seemingly hostile city has been to find succour in satire. Certainly the pretensions and foibles of the citizens have often deserved to be held up for ridicule, although it is open to question whether doing so has provided much comfort for misanthropic

The Central Catholic Library (above) is a voluntary subscription library, as were nearly all such institutions until the end of the 19th century. Occupying a fine Georgian house in Merrion Square, the library is funded by members' subscriptions and its own limited resources. Founded in other premises in 1922 by a Jesuit priest,

Fr Stephen Browne, the CCL moved to its present home eleven years later. Among its more unusual characteristics is the fact that the collection of some 100,000 volumes has been catalogued not by the customary Dewey system, but by a form of classification used in medieval libraries and still in use in the Vatican Library.

The book collection of Trinity College runs to several million, but the majority of works are stored elsewhere in the city. Some of the oldest and most valuable volumes owned by the college can be seen on the shelves of its 18th-century Old Library building (right).

authors. Dublin's foremost satirist was perhaps her first, Jonathan Swift, the troubled Dean of St Patrick's Cathedral who was buried within its walls, 'where savage indignation can no longer lacerate his breast'. He once wrote to Esther Vanhomrigh, otherwise known as Vanessa, 'I ever feared the tattle of this nasty town,' but while he sometimes felt the need to excoriate the population of Dublin, more usually his spleen was vented against the British government which showed such poor understanding of Ireland and her particular circumstances. Among the most notorious work was *A Modest Proposal*, a pamphlet published in 1729 suggesting, with all semblance of seriousness, that the best means to solve the country's economic misfortunes was for the poor to eat their own children, thereby dispensing with the need to provide any other food for them.

Swift's most obvious successor, in terms of both personal character and literary style, was Brian O'Nolan, better known as Flann O'Brien, who for over twenty-five years from 1940 wrote a humorous column for

The *Irish Times* newspaper under yet another name, Myles na gCopaleen. In these pieces the affectations and pomposities of mid-20th century Dublin suffered an assault from which they were unable to recover, terminally wounded by O'Nolan's mastery of language and awareness of how the absurd can be discovered in the supposedly ordinary. Although born in Northern Ireland, O'Nolan possessed an acute ear for the argot of Dublin, reproduced and enriched in a number of his novels including the first, *At Swim-Two-Birds* (1939) which was inspired by the work of another writer from the capital, James Joyce.

Brian O'Nolan died in 1966, appropriately enough on April Fools' Day, his latter years soured by an excessive intake of alcohol, much of it consumed in the Palace Bar near the offices of *The Irish Times*. *At Swim-Two-Birds* contains a poem 'A pint of plain is your only man', to be recited in this pub. But the truth is that despite their dominant presence in the lives of many Dublin writers, such hostelries have rarely contributed much benefit to the city's literary heritage. The poet Patrick Kavanagh once wrote of a man in London longing to return to Dublin, 'Where among the failures he would pass unnoticed / Happy in pubs talking about yesterday's wits / And George Moore's use of the semi-colon.' Many great books have gone unwritten in Dublin's pubs, their pages talked away over a succession of drinks, leaving the putative author with nothing other than an empty pocket and a sore head.

Nevertheless, certain bars in the city have managed to acquire and retain a 'literary' reputation perhaps because, as Benedict Kiely has observed of Dublin, while books could be read, 'going to the pubs was easier

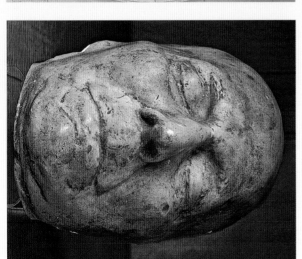

Most writers associated with Dublin have now had their memory preserved in a piece of sculpture. In the park of St Stephen's Green, for example, there are monuments to Joyce, Yeats, Mangan and Thomas Kettle, a poet killed during the First World War. Oddly enough, although he lived in the adjacent Newman House, there is no acknowledgment given here to the English poet and Jesuit priest Gerard Manley Hopkins, possibly because he was miserable throughout the five years he spent in the city, dying there in 1889. 'Dublin,' he wrote to his friend Robert Bridges, 'is a joyless place.'

Actually, the want of joy was more on Hopkins' part than on Dublin's, a place in which he forever felt alien. But that condition has never been exclusive to those born far from the place. It seems clear that in adulthood Samuel Beckett was uncomfortable in his native city and while he taught at his Alma Mater, Trinity College, for a year, he rarely returned to Dublin after moving to France in the 1930s. However, Dublin appears in his work, most overtly in the 1934 collection of short stories, *More Pricks than Kicks* which follows the life of a Trinity College student called Belacqua Shuah.

It is even more ironic that Dublin's most significant chronicler should have spent the greater part of his life far away from the city. James Joyce preferred to recall Dublin at a distance, mapping out its streets in his memory and reordering them to suit his literary purposes. Joyce – and through him all Dublin's writers – is now annually commemorated in the capital on 16 June, otherwise known as Bloomsday after Leopold Bloom, the central figure of *Ulysses* who spent that day in 1904 on a peregrination around the city.

It was in 1904 that Joyce definitively left Dublin, returning there for the last time in 1912. Two years after that, his first prose book was published, called *Dubliners*, a collection of fifteen short stories set in the city of his birth, which, he said, seemed to him the centre of paralysis. This view of Dublin was obviously to soften the longer Joyce stayed away and, although this attitude is still apparent in *A Portrait of the Artist as a Young Man* (1916), it is far less evident in *Ulysses*, first published in 1922.

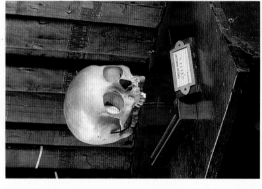

The first public library in Ireland was opened in 1707 thanks to the beneficence of Dublin's Archbishop Narcissus Marsh (above and right). Designed by Sir William Robinson, its interior remains almost unchanged and is still open to the public. The dark oak carved bookcases, holding a collection of some 25,000 volumes, are each topped with a bishop's mitre and there are also three wire 'cages' in which readers consulting particularly valuable work were traditionally locked for the duration of their stay. The skull is that of Dean Swift's friend Esther Johnson, otherwise known as Stella, who died in 1728.

Kavanagh himself, according to the author Anthony Cronin who knew him well, used to drink in The Palace on Fleet Street, where he would sit, 'entranced in the inner circle of the local world of letters'. Today he is commemorated by a statue of himself seated on a bench next to the Grand Canal. Nearby is Herbert Place, where Elizabeth Bowen spent the first years of her childhood, commemorated by her in *Seven Winters*, while other writers associated with this quiet residential quarter of the city include Liam O'Flaherty and Thomas Davis, a poet and one of the leaders of the Young Ireland movement who himself died young at the age of just thirty. There is much melancholy associated with the poets of Dublin, but also much joy, these two characteristics found in equal measure throughout the work of W.B. Yeats. After a peripatetic youth, Yeats spent most of his adult life in the city, along with his much admired friend and fellow-author George Russell, known as A.E., who 'was the nearest to a saint you or I will ever meet,' Mrs Yeats once told her husband, adding, 'You are a better poet, but no saint.'

Sanctity is not necessarily a quality found among writers. But neither is gloom, and some of the poets associated with Dublin inspire more cheer than others. Certainly, Thomas Moore, who was born at 12 Aungier Street, brought glory to himself and pleasure to his readers through the verses he wrote. The close companion of Lord Byron, he was also, according to Lady Morgan, 'the guest of princes and the friend of peers'.

and much more fun.' Among the venues frequented by those in search of the city's authors, past and present, is McDaid's on Harry Street, a bar associated with Brendan Behan who frequently brought his typewriter to the premises so that he could simultaneously write and drink. Not too far away still stands Davy Byrne's on Duke Street, the 'moral pub' immortalized by Joyce in *Ulysses*. Directly opposite is The Bailey, now bearing absolutely no resemblance to the premises that formerly contained the doorway of Bloom's supposed home on Eccles Street – when this item was originally installed in the pub, Patrick Kavanagh declared it, 'Now Shut!'

LITERARY
BIJOU

The devotion of Dubliners to books is epitomized by the home of Patrick Bowe and his wife Nicola Gordon Bowe. The Bowes share a house in the Dublin district of Ranelagh with their daughter, their dogs and, of course, a collection of books running to thousands. Both of them are writers, he specializing in gardens, she in art history, but their reading interests spread far beyond these areas to cover an eclectic range of subjects.

'We're inclusive and not exclusive in any way,' Nicola Gordon Bowe explains. 'Everything in the house has a resonance, has a reason for being collected – for its colour or form or the reason it was first bought or given to us.'

The Bowe taste is definitely not minimalist. The couple love to display an enormous collection of objects and art works which have come from places as diverse as their appearance: eastern Europe, India and Central America. Despite this diversity, the house's decoration is not discordant, but often brought together by a common colour palette. Furthermore, says Nicola Gordon Bowe, 'I love the resonances everything we have brings back; the idea of material memory is very important. Everything here sets up a train of thought.'

Central to all these treasures are books, found in great piles in every room of the Bowe household. Any available wall is lined with bookshelves and no surface has been left uncovered by a spill of straying volumes. Visitors to the house can sometimes find even tracing a clear seat difficult. 'They're our familiars,' comments Nicola Gordon Bowe. 'Of course they're the everyday tools of our trade for both of us in our work, but they're not just repositories of information; they're demarcations of knowledge as well.'

Strong colours and bold patterns are evident throughout the home of Patrick and Nicola Bowe (these and following pages). For reasons of work and personal interest alike, both are indefatigable travellers and their journeys have always yielded treasures to be brought back to the house where, somehow, space must be found for their display. Just as the couple mix a wide variety of subjects in their extensive book collection, so they have no qualms in juxtaposing work from different parts of the world. 'I don't believe in putting things away inside cupboards,' she says, 'especially not books. Of course I can never find what I'm looking for when I need it, but I love them all dearly.'

What might Joyce have thought of the manner in which the city he spurned – and which in turn spurned him – has embraced this writer since his death? There are more memorials and tributes to him than to any other author in Dublin. Indeed, he has an entire building devoted to his memory at 35 North Great George's Street. In the writer's lifetime, this was a dancing academy run by one Dennis Maginni who appears under his own name in *Ulysses*. It is now the James Joyce Cultural Centre and beneath the neoclassical ceilings can be found a wide variety of memorabilia relating to the man, his life and work.

As if this were not sufficient tribute, in the coastal suburb of Sandycove can be found a Joyce Museum located in a fortified tower dating from the early 19th century. Joyce lived here very briefly in 1904 and would later commemorate the experience, together with his host Oliver St John Gogarty, in *Ulysses*, where the latter is given the fictional guise of Buck Mulligan. In addition, visitors to Dublin can seek out 'Ulysses Trails' and statues to Joyce. All this attention devoted by the city to one writer, albeit her most important, threatens to overwhelm all the others and many of Joyce's successors understandably claim to be intimidated by his abiding influence. Furthermore, some of Joyce's forebears no longer receive as much attention as they did prior to the ascent of his reputation. This probably irritates their admirers but they ought not to feel too resentful. Joyce's fiction is replete with references, some more oblique to others, to the writers who had gone before them. *Ulysses* in particular, offers readers not just a map of Dublin but also a guide to the city's literary history.

Designed by Thomas Burgh, the long room of Trinity College's Old Library (right) was begun in 1719 while the main room of the Royal Irish Academy (overleaf) dates from more than two centuries later. Both are of considerable interest to scholars.

SOCIAL

Dublin's citizens have a well-deserved reputation for entertaining loquaciousness and one of the principal pleasures for any visitor to the city is meeting its residents. There are many opportunities to do this, thanks to the wealth of sporting, social and cultural occasions to which Dublin plays host.

Bachelors Walk, a place where Dubliners have been meeting for centuries.

'The address of an Irish beggar is much more poetical and animated than that of an English one,' wrote a visitor to Dublin in the early 19th century. That poetry and animation have never been exclusive either to one period or class but remain just as much in evidence in Irish society today. It is a well-established axiom that the people of Ireland love to talk and, as a result, have elevated not just conversation but the art of conviviality to a peculiarly high plane. In their capital, evidence of this widespread delight in companionable talk can easily be discovered. Unlike many other cities, Dublin social life is a very public affair; the streets and bars are her salons where the issues of the moment – from the political scandals that are a constant feature of Irish life to the contested results of a major sporting event – will be debated and analyzed.

Conversation in Ireland has always been a competitive, even combative, undertaking. The late actor and writer Micheal MacLiammoir once observed that the reason Oscar Wilde moved to England was that, had he remained in Dublin, the rest of the population would have been constantly tempted 'either to cap or capsise' his witticisms. Participants in the city's social life are advised to possess mental agility and verbal dexterity.

For the non-native, however, traditionally the most striking characteristic of the local population has been its relaxed and sociable charm. Intense sociability is a long-standing feature of Dubliners. Can it be any accident that, when the Norsemen established the city over a thousand years ago, one of their first acts was to create an official meeting place, the Thingmote? Perhaps its tradition lingers on in some of the larger bars and clubs, the new social meeting places, which have opened around the capital during recent years.

'Blarney' may be a word derived from a castle in County Cork, but its presence can just as easily be discovered in Dublin. There is a term in the Gaelic language, *plamas*, implying flattery and fascination, which suggests that linguistic charm is an inherent trait of the national temperament. The link widely made between Ireland and entertaining conversation can also

The proverbial pint of plain (above): the drink which has been associated with Dublin, and her social life, for centuries. It is best consumed in one of the city's fine collection of traditional pubs (right and overleaf) where time – like the clock on the wall – seems to have stood still for as long as anyone can remember. Drinking in Dublin can be a communal or a solitary activity depending on the venue and the time of day; wherever and whenever, there is always companionship to be found in a pint.

be held responsible for the Irish pub concept: a global export based on the notion that a place of public association will become more convivial if it can claim a connection with a nation of charming talkers.

Dublin's pubs, of course, have been at the centre of the city's social life for centuries and remain so today. There are now more than 700 such premises in the capital and especially on weekend nights they all seem to be full to the point of discomfort. The traditional reputation of the capital's pubs is that they are places where the repartee flows as smoothly as the drink. It does not take long to disabuse anyone of this fanciful notion because, in a crowded and noisy venue, even the most amusing of remarks is likely to pass unheard. Meanwhile, a quiet bar is more likely to resemble the melancholy premises depicted in Conor McPherson's play *The Weir* than a spot where amusing banter is tossed about between staff and clientele. A barstool bore is as likely to be encountered in Dublin as anywhere else, so engaging a neighbour in conversation carries risks.

With those provisos understood, a night – or several – in one of the city's pubs can still be an agreeably social experience, particularly if it is passed in the company of native Dubliners. Despite all the changes the capital has undergone in the last few years, certain premises have managed to retain both their character and appearance. Pre-eminent among these is the Horseshoe Bar in the Shelbourne Hotel into which, on most evenings of the week, but especially Fridays, a substantial cross-section of Dublin society squeezes to trade news, views, compliments and insults. Something of a national institution for more than half a century, the Horseshoe is just one of a number of venues which are claimed by their admirers to be the real centre of government in Ireland – a measure of the important status given to pubs by the capital's residents. Doheny & Nesbitt, a mere stagger from the Shelbourne Hotel on Lower Baggot Street, is another spot where the nation's decision-makers, real or self-proclaimed, are known to gather. But for outsiders, the more obvious appeal of this bar will be its fine old interior, the wood panelling

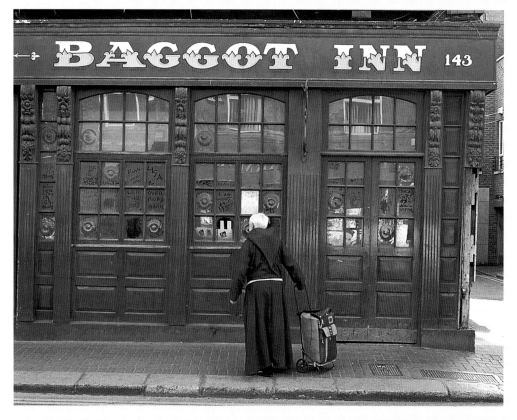

ripe from absorbing decades of nicotine and alcohol fumes, as well as conversation inspired by both.

It should be stated that abundant talk is not an indispensable attribute for Dublin pubs. There can be conviviality in silence or in music. Traditional Irish music has much of the same springing rhythm and lyricism as Irish speech; it would be natural to find a connection between the two forms of communication and one often takes the place of the other in Dublin's bars. O'Donoghue's on Merrion Row south of the river and the Cobblestone in Smithfield on the northside are two of the best places in which to find the country's traditional music. Few subjects bring strangers together better than a shared interest, which explains why these pubs are cherished for their music and sociability alike.

There are a number of other wonderful old bars in the city centre, the owners of which have resisted the temptation to extend or modernize their premises, a blight which saw the destruction of many Dublin landmarks during the heady days of the 1990s. Among the most appealing such places are the Long Hall on South Great George's Street; the International Bar on Wicklow Street; the Palace on Fleet Street; the Stag's Head on Dame Court; and Mulligan's of Poolbeg Street. All have retained their original décor and, looking at the age of some of the drinkers, possibly their original clientele as well. It is a feature of the city's older premises that as far as possible their design excludes the outside world. Windows are small and few, little natural light is permitted to enter the interior, its décor of varnished mahogany and polished brass bears almost no comparison with anywhere else. The effect is to enclose the customer in an enticing environment, one where the exertions of daily existence can, at least temporarily, be forgotten. Nothing often happens in the

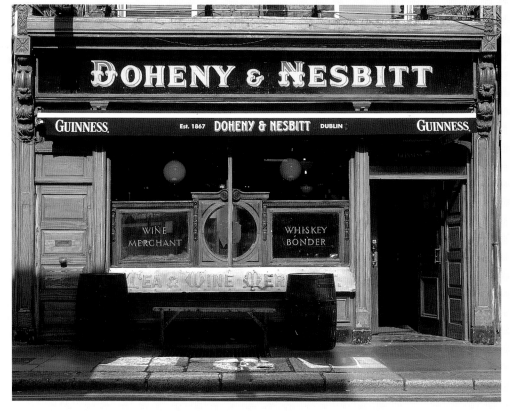

Despite the arrival of new pubs aimed at the younger and more fashion-conscious consumer, there are still plenty of old premises to be discovered in Dublin, such as the Baggot Inn and its near neighbour Doheny & Nesbitt, both on Baggot Street (left), O'Neill's on Suffolk Street (right), The Long Hall on South Great George's Street and The Old Stand on Exchequer Street (overleaf).

city's pubs and in this circumstance lies their dangerous allure. Nothing perhaps except some meandering conversation in which ideas and fancies are given more attention and credence than they deserve.

Such are the snares of Dublin pubs, but blessedly the city has many other places in which to meet and socialize. Although alcohol is served in hotels such as the Shelbourne and the Merrion, so are less overtly intoxicating drinks like tea and coffee. Indeed, tea rather than stout might almost be considered the national beverage, so widely is it consumed and in such quantities.

The city's most famous supplier of coffee and tea alike is Bewley's Oriental Café, a chain that opened its first premises in the late 19th century. Aficionados of Bewley's will claim that the company's outlets are not what they once were, but then again what is, especially in a city that has undergone as much change of late as Dublin? But regardless of any transformations it has experienced, the principal Bewley's premises on Grafton Street retains its status as an important focal point for locals and visitors alike.

The impression may now have been given that social life in Dublin revolves around drink, alcoholic or otherwise, consumed in snug premises, and even a passing familiarity with the dank Irish climate would certainly encourage that notion. Nevertheless, centuries of facing into wind and rain have made Dubliners a hardy breed and so they are also prepared to take advantage of the open spaces available to them. Many of these are devoted to the large variety of sports played in the city, among the most popular – and sociable – being racing. The other major equestrian occasion associated with the capital is the Horse Show, held in the grounds of the Royal Dublin Society for a week every August, culminating on Friday with the international competition among show jumpers for the Aga Khan Trophy.

Just off Grafton Street, a bar's clientele spills out onto the adjacent pavement. This is a relatively new phenomenon in Dublin; traditionally drinkers stayed indoors where warmth and comfort was assured. The city's climate has certainly not improved of late, but perhaps its residents have become hardier.

SOCIAL
ELEGANT

'I love being in the centre of the city,' says one of Ireland's most renowned fashion designers, Louise Kennedy. 'This is actually a very quiet location at weekends.' The location in question is a five-storey, late-18th-century house on the south side of Dublin's Merrion Square where Kennedy has lived and worked since 1998. Her home accommodates her office as well as the city's smallest department store; three distinct functions reflecting the same design philosophy.

Louise Kennedy summarizes her work as offering 'understated elegance and relaxed simplicity.' These qualities are reflected throughout her Merrion Square house, from the basement design studio to the open-plan living space which the designer created for herself on the top floor. She points out that one advantageous feature found everywhere in the building is an abundance of natural light, helped by the central glass-topped stairwell that runs through the core of the property. In addition, the main rooms benefit from high ceilings and long windows which help to bring the outside indoors.

'I deliberately chose a neutral palette with slightly different colour washes running through the house,' Kennedy explains, 'so one room naturally leads to the next with a common handwriting. There's a very calming aura everywhere.' That sense of calm is particularly evident at weekends, when Merrion Square becomes quiet. The park on her doorstep 'gives me a sense of living in the countryside thanks to the tranquility and the wonderful views I can get from all the windows on the front of the house.' The view from the back of the house is just as appealing since it stretches all the way to the distant Dublin Mountains.

A series of small ground-floor rooms at the front of the house was opened up by Louise Kennedy to create an elegant and spacious entrance hall (left). Similarly, her need for light and space led the designer to remove all divisions on the building's top floor in order to make one big gallery centred around the glass-topped stairwell (above). The room is now big enough to serve as Kennedy's private entertaining area where she often holds dinners for friends (overleaf).

Successfully in business since the mid-1980s, Kennedy bought this property so that she could find an outlet for her interest in areas of design other than fashion. In 1999 she teamed up with Tipperary Crystal to create a range of glass and tableware. The venture has proven both stimulating for her and commercially advantageous; Kennedy now sees herself moving into other areas of home design such as bed and table linen.

The designer's own seasonal lines of women's clothing are on sale in the house's first-floor rooms; her list of customers ranges from Ireland's first woman president Mary Robinson (who wore a Louise Kennedy design for her inauguration) to Meryl Streep, Irish singer Enya and the Countess of Wessex. Kennedy also stocks work by a number of other designers, such as Philip Treacy and Lulu Guinness, along with furnishings by the likes of David Linley. Elsewhere can be found items brought back from her travels around the globe, such as the five figures of Buddha greeting all visitors in the entrance hall. Like everything else in the house, they conform to Louise Kennedy's impeccable standards of taste.

Three times winner of the Irish Designer of the Year award, Louise Kennedy's clothes reflect her own preference for understated elegance and clean shapes (above). The same taste is also found in the ranges of glassware she has designed for Tipperary Crystal, such as the fruit bowl on the table in her private living room and the candlesticks on the mantelpiece (right).

The designer's choice of furnishings reflects her constant travels as well as her diverse sources of inspiration. Her refined eye allows her to mix pieces picked up in Southeast Asia and India with Irish and English work from the 18th and 19th centuries. Mixed together with confidence, all look comfortably at home within the same Georgian house.

The national sports of Ireland are hurling and Gaelic football, both of them supervised by the Gaelic Athletic Association which since 1913 has had its headquarters at Croke Park in Dublin's northern inner suburbs. Both games are specific to the country and only acquired their present formal rules following the establishment of the G.A.A. in the 1880s. Hurling is an extremely ancient game, dating back to pre-Christian Ireland and mentioned in the legend of Cuchulainn. While not as old, Gaelic football, which looks like a cross between soccer and rugby, although it predates both, has been played for many centuries; the first reported match took place in 1712 in Meath when that county played against its neighbour Louth. One of the men responsible for the G.A.A.'s creation, Michael Cusack, is caricatured by James Joyce in *Ulysses*, but as a rule the organization is held in high esteem throughout Ireland. Large sections of the rural population descend on Dublin for inter-county and important club matches at Croke Park, as well as the annual all-Ireland hurling finals which are held on the first Sunday in September followed by the Gaelic football final a fortnight later. Despite being redeveloped, the stadium still proves too small to meet the demand for tickets.

Football and hurling, may be Ireland's offical games, but soccer is probably the sport with the greatest following throughout the country, including Dublin. The capital remains home to several teams participating in the National League run by the Football Association of Ireland: among the most popular are Shelbourne, Bohemians and Shamrock Rovers. But despite soccer's wide fanbase, it has no large stadium and international matches must be played in the Lansdowne Road premises lent for the occasion by the Irish Rugby Football Union.

Just as the rich and poor live in close proximity to one another, so shopping in Dublin has always been a mixture of the exclusive and the popular. Here, on a little side street in the city centre, a gourmet food outlet stands next to a premises offering discount fabrics and another selling second-hand clothes; the same customers are likely to visit all three.

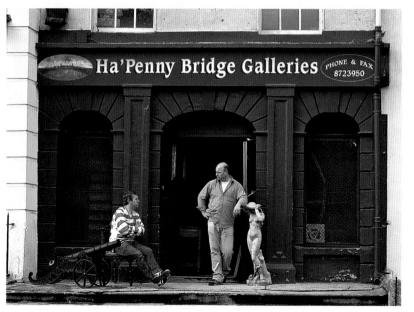

The traditional Irish shopfront has long been one of the country's delights, found in towns and cities, small and large alike. In their original form, they consisted of a large wood or glass fascia, handpainted with details of the owner's name and profession. These would be framed by pilasters with elaborately carved capitals. The colours used to paint the finished work were often very bright, as though in defiance of the grey Irish skyline and distinctive forms of lettering were developed for the shopfronts, as the familiar Antique Roman typeface underwent a variety of modifications.

Sadly, although they survive in relatively large numbers elsewhere around Ireland, many of the capital's old retail façades were destroyed during the course of the economic boom as widespread redevelopment took place. The craftsmen who specialized in their creation have also almost entirely disappeared. Those that remain are now much appreciated and even emulated by some of the newer premises which have opened in Dublin in recent years.

Like any family with young children, Amanda Pratt and her husband Tom Kelly spend much of their time at home in the kitchen. Despite being in the basement of the house, this one is particularly light and airy, reflecting Pratt's belief in the importance of these qualities. 'Living in Ireland,' she says, 'we don't have much sunshine and suffer from so much greyness, light is a hugely important thing for us. I can't bear heavy curtains or anything which detracts from getting natural light.' Her preference for simple elegance is also apparent, even in the kitchen. 'I'd prefer to sit in a beautiful room than a comfortable one,' she remarks.

'I do almost all my design work for Avoca Handweavers at home either at night or at the weekends,' Amanda Pratt confesses. Nevertheless, she and her husband still find the time to entertain friends who willingly cluster around this dining table for lunches and suppers. Besides, such occasions provide an opportunity to see what fresh alterations their hostess has made to her home. 'I do like moving furniture around and seeing how it looks,' she says. 'I think it's important to be able to change and be relaxed about enjoying your home.' This is a case of the house as a work in progress.

SOCIAL
FEMININE

Design Director for her family's highly successful retail business, Avoca Handweavers, Amanda Pratt lives with her husband Tom Kelly and their twin daughters in a handsome house dating from around 1830 at Monkstown ,on the south Dublin coast, a short distance from the city centre. Her home reflects her refined tastes and, she admits, often acts as a laboratory for the designs later found in the company's outlets.

Since moving into this house in 1994, Amanda Pratt has introduced an abundance of colour and light, as well as an intriguing blend of furniture, such as that found in her two daughters' bedrooms. 'For me,' she comments, 'a room must be visually comfortable first of all.' Other than light muslin drapes, the house is devoid of curtains. Its floors are stripped and varnished and the walls left almost unadorned so that the fine pre-Victorian interiors can be properly appreciated.

When the Temple Bar district of central Dublin was restored during the 1990s, entire new squares and streets were created in the area. And with them came opportunities for new commercial activities such as the food market held every Saturday in Meeting House Square. Both the venue and most of the goods on offer are innovative in character, Dubliners until now not being used to jams made from obscure organic fruits or more than a dozen different varieties of sausage. But they have proved remarkably adaptable in the face of these unusual foods which, along with more regular produce such as cabbages, onions and lettuce, sell in healthy abundance each weekend. And, of course, the other feature of the Meeting House Market is its sociability, helped by a plentiful supply of restaurants and cafés in the immediate vicinity.

Aspiring young footballers can be seen practising their skills in Dublin's many parks, frequently even in those where the playing of such games is officially forbidden. The greatest of these open spaces is the Phoenix Park, now almost 350 years old. Once on the periphery of the true city, it has become an essential green lung for the capital, surrounded by concentrated residential areas. Dubliners use the park for many purposes. Within its boundaries are contained a number of different sporting facilities, such as a polo ground, and during the summer, matches here are important social occasions. Joggers, walkers, strollers, amblers: they all abound in the park's 1,752 acres, which comfortably absorbed over a million people in 1979 when Pope John Paul II held an open-air service there.

Whilst always important to Dublin's residents, the Phoenix Park seems not to have played much of a role in their social lives; it never had the same cachet as once did London's Hyde Park or the Bois du Boulogne in Paris. On the other hand, St Stephen's Green, almost from the moment it was first created, became the place in which to be seen by other members of fashionable society. In the 18th century, the northside of the park contained a promenade known as Beaux' Walk and the houses built around it were occupied by prominant members of the peerage and parliament.

Since being given to the people of Dublin by Lord Ardilaun in 1877, the green has been open to all members of the public, but not far away is the last park exclusive only to owners and residents of the surrounding properties, that at the centre of Fitzwilliam Square. The same used to be the case for the adjacent Merrion Square but its landscaped grounds are now freely accessible. Running to almost 12 acres, the square's park was bought in 1930 by the Roman Catholic church, but ceded it to the city authorities forty-four years later.

Dublin's oldest and most famous open-air market can be found on the northside of the city on Moore Street. Unlike its more recently established rival in Temple Bar, this one does not specialize in organic food. Indeed, it concentrates on little other than consistently low prices.

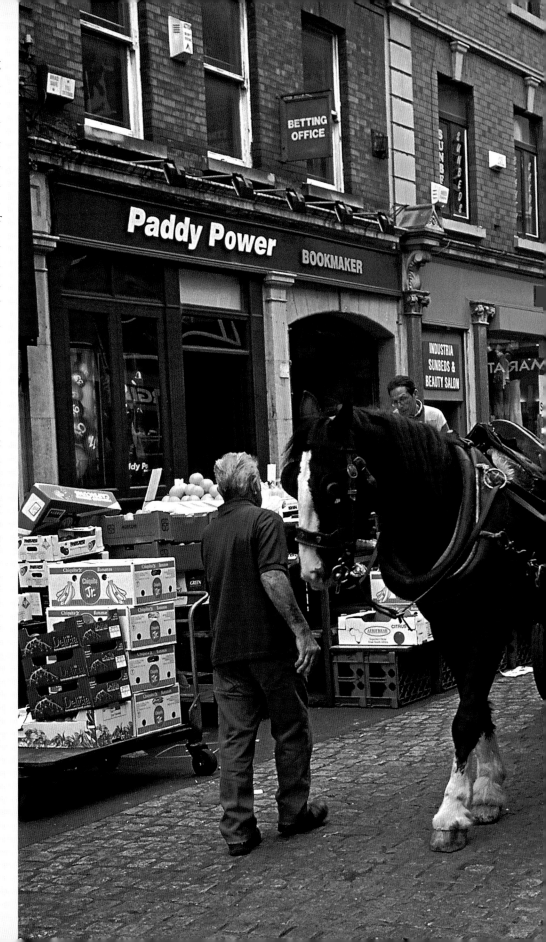

SOCIAL
GARDEN

Dublin's most celebrated garden has been created by
someone who is not a Dubliner but who is unques-
tionably a great gardener, Scottish-born Helen
Dillon. The pretty terraced house she shares with her
husband Val, an antiques consultant, dates from
around 1830. The main garden behind is of much
more recent vintage and, unlike the building, is also
in a state of constant flux as new ideas and plants are
introduced with each season.

The Dillons moved to their home in 1972 and for the
first year they concentrated on making it habitable.
Only gradually was attention paid to the garden. Initially, insists Mrs Dillon, she was timid about altering
anything within the grounds and shrunk from remov-
ing any plants that had already taken root. But over the
intervening three decades, she has grown progressively
bolder and now says she has no qualms about pulling
up anything which no longer takes her fancy.

'I'm always remaking the place,' she comments. 'If
you do something and then just have it there to be
looked after and maintained, it's like living in a
museum.' Mrs Dillon travels regularly to lecture on
gardens, usually visiting the United States every spring
and autumn, as well as going on plant hunting trips to
destinations such as the Himalayas, the Alps and South
Africa. 'It's a good way of seeing other people's gardens,'
she says, 'and not letting yourself get stuck in a rut.'

To avoid this, she constantly reorders different sections of her own garden. The greatest change in recent
years has been the removal of the central lawn behind

*The wild ducks seen next to the canal in Val and Helen Dillon's backgarden are
annual visitors. 'There are two males and a female,' Mrs Dillon remarks.
'They come in April and go at the end of June for the mating season;
we're very used to seeing them here with us.'*

the house and its replacement with a shallow canal in late 2000. Although inspired by visits to Morocco and the Alhambra Palace in Granada, Mrs Dillons recalls, 'I used to claim I wanted a canal as a joke. But then the lawn was driving us potty because it took gallons of water and had to be fed every ten days and mown twice a week during the summer. But the main thing was that I wanted the sparkle of water. It's so bright and exciting, even in winter, I love looking at it. We get very low levels of light in this country – the same as Newfoundland – so this is a way to increase the sense of light and the movement of light.' In her usual forthright manner, Mrs Dillon explains the canal's size, 'I wanted lots of water for water's sake; not for two goldfish and a lily.'

Further changes have taken place and more are planned. The north-facing front garden was given an overhaul in 1996 and could be changed again. And the raised beds flanking the Irish limestone around the new canal are about to be transformed. 'For too many years,' Mrs Dillon observes, 'people have been making theme gardens around colours…I'm going to break up all that red and blue colour theme. Now I want to put in oranges and yellows with it.' The Dillon garden is open to the public in spring and summer and visitors need to return regularly to witness its fresh transformations.

Mrs Dillon's desire for constant change means that the deep beds shown here will soon look very different. Even garden structures are not immune to her attention: the finial-topped summer house seen to the left was entirely rebuilt in 1998.

One of a terrace of handsome houses in Ranelagh, a former village on the outskirts of central Dublin, the Dillon home dates from around 1830 (above). Its north-facing front garden is, according to Mrs Dillon, difficult to plant successfully but she has managed to overcome the challenge. Inside the house, her fondness for innovation can be seen in the ground-floor lavatory (right), the walls of which were entirely decorated with seashells over a two-week period in 2000 by the English artist Blot Kerr-Wilson; the shells came from a wide variety of sources including France, India and the United States.

The Dillons' drawing room has also recently been overhauled (far right). 'It's important to clear things out,' explains its chatelaine. Some of the furniture here she inherited, but the portrait of a girl over the fireplace 'isn't a relation. We have it because we thought she has a nice dress.'

Does it seem strange, even sacrilegious, to refer to churches when speaking of social life in Dublin? But for a long time, until the recent decline in religious practice, these buildings were central to the lives of the capital's citizens. Especially while another state governed the country, attendance at Roman Catholic churches was an expression not just of religious faith but also political belief. The majority of the population in Dublin, as elsewhere throughout Ireland, remained Catholic even through the centuries when to be so risked incurring severe penalties.

Given that Ireland has long been renowned for its devotion to Catholicism, it may strike visitors as odd that there should be no Catholic cathedral in the capital, especially when much smaller centres of population around the country can claim such structures. The explanation for this state of affairs lies in the tortured religious history of Ireland. Until independence was achieved in the 1920s, the state faith was that imposed by the British authorities who, at the time of the Reformation, took control of Dublin's two cathedrals, St Patrick's and Christchurch. Legislation meant that the Catholic faith could not be practised publicly until 1829, although even before that date construction had begun on a temporary or Pro-Cathedral which still stands on Marlborough Street.

For the poor of Dublin – of which there have always been a great many – churches served as a manifestation of the country's collective wealth. There are, therefore, some splendid places of worship found even in the most abject districts of the city, the majority built during the post-Catholic emancipation decades of the 19th century, but a couple pre-date that period. It is worth seeking out the church of the Discalced Carmelites on Clarendon Street, for example. Although subsequently expanded, it was first built on a laneway in

As far back as the 1670s, Sir William Temple wrote that 'horses in Ireland are a drug', and little has changed in the intervening centuries. Since the closure of the racecourse next to the Phoenix Park, that at Leopardstown is nearest to the centre of Dublin.

Leopardstown racecourse opened to the public in 1888 on land which had been set aside for housing development by a pair of speculators. When their ambitious scheme foundered, part of the site was used to create this sporting venue. As a testament to the Irish love of horses, Leopardstown's success was immediate; so many people turned up for the first meeting that local resources such as transport could not cope. Traffic jams remain the norm as punters flock

to the course, especially for the annual three-day event immediately after Christmas. Race meetings around Dublin are egalitarian occasions at which all classes of the city's society mingle. Although Leopardstown racecourse now has extremely smart facilities for private dining (and drinking, this being Ireland after all), even so rich and poor citizens alike will be found sharing the same interest in events on the course.

In ancient Irish mythology, the warrior Fionn MacCumhaill and his followers, the Fianna, were said to have raced against each other across the Curragh outside Dublin, home to another of the country's finest racecourses. Ardent followers of the sport, of which there are many in Ireland, would claim the same legendary status for more recent meetings at Leopardstown, which stages both flat- and hunt-racing events throughout the year during the course of a busy programme. Regulars at the course will often be serious betters on successive races as large amounts of money are gambled during the course of an afternoon. A day at Leopardstown provides an excellent opportunity to see Dublin society at its most intense, engaged and impassioned — and all because of a handful of horses.

the 1790s, when such buildings were officially forbidden. A tour of Dublin's palatial Catholic churches would have to include St Andrew's on Westland Row – Daniel O'Connell encouraged its construction and worshipped there – as well as St Audoen's on High Street and the Franciscan Church on Merchant's Quay; the last of these is familiarly known as Adam and Eve's. The great Catholic church architect during the first half of the 19th century was Patrick Byrne, of whom little is known except that he clearly ran a highly successful practice. Among his other works is St Paul's on Arran Quay.

Nevertheless, the Church of Ireland continues to possess if not the largest then certainly the most beautiful places of worship in Dublin, including her two medieval cathedrals. Both were heavily, perhaps too heavily, restored in the Victorian era but during the previous century the state faith built for itself some exquisite churches. Many still open today, such as St Ann's on Dawson Street where, behind a mid-19th century neo-Romanesque façade lies a perfectly preserved galleried interior dating from the 1720s. Then there is St Werburgh's, constructed around the same period and retaining its original Georgian internal decoration. Unfortunately, the fine spire added in 1768 was taken down forty-odd years later because there were fears it could be used by potential rebels to shoot at the occupants of Dublin Castle behind the church.

For a wide variety of reasons, churches – whether those belonging to the Catholic or Church of Ireland congregations – have ceased to hold their traditionally important place in Dublin's social hierarchy. Given Ireland's troubled religious history, perhaps this altered status is beneficial, but one consequence has been that a large number of buildings formerly used for services are now closed or converted to other purposes. Dublin, however, is not unused to radical change, having undergone metamorphosis on a number of previous occasions. So the closure and conversion of churches is just one element of the city transforming herself into another guise.

The large public square at the centre of the Smithfield district on the northside of Dublin was established as a market in the 17th century. More recently, it served as a monthly horse fair, where animals unlikely ever to appear at any of the country's prestigious racecourses were bought and sold. Although now moved out of the square, which is being redeveloped as part of an urban renewal scheme, the horse fair continues to take place on nearby Morningstar Avenue. What makes it notable is that most of the purchasers and vendors live within the city, keeping their horses in back gardens or on common land outside residential complexes and riding them around the streets of Dublin.

CONTEMPORARY

Dublin today bears almost no resemblance to the city bearing the same name little more than ten years ago. During the final decade of the twentieth century, a new sense of self-confidence and an improved economy allowed Ireland's capital to transform herself into a more vibrant place than had been the case for almost two hundred years.

Fireworks over the River Liffey mark St Patrick's Day.

In the early 1990s, something strange happened in Dublin; the city suddenly and unexpectedly became fashionable. International magazines took to describing the Irish capital as the 'coolest,' 'hippest' and most exciting place on the planet. Initially, Dubliners observed this change of circumstance with bemusement. After all, for generations their city had been considered shabby rather than chic, faded instead of fashionable. How could it be that Dublin, in the eyes of the global community, was suddenly perceived as a glamorous holiday destination, when to her own residents she had long been dear but dirty, run-down and irredeemably unstylish?

Yet the global status of Dublin did fundamentally change towards the close of the twentieth century. Many of today's visitors to the city probably have no interest in her Georgian architecture or her remarkable literary roll-call. Instead, they have come to Dublin to experience her contemporary character. And specifically to enjoy some of that distinctive – if elusive – Irish quality known as 'craic.' Pronounced 'crack' and therefore liable to be misunderstood, this is a Gaelic term that has come to summarize a sociable good time in Ireland. Craic is much sought, although not always found, by visitors to Dublin. But whether they discover it or not, what remains remarkable is that cheerfulness, optimism and buoyancy are now traits associated with the city instead of the melancholy and gloom which were traditionally thought to be her principal characteristics.

The large number of tourists choosing to visit the city need somewhere to stay, and so, since the mid-1990s, there has been a veritable explosion of hotel-building. From having scarcely any bedrooms for guests barely twenty years ago, Dublin now has thousands.

Traffic surges along the quays of Dublin at night. There have been many advantages to the city's recent economic boom, but also a few drawbacks, one of them being the enormous increase in vehicles attempting to move through the city centre.

The old and the new juxtaposed in
contemporary Dublin. In the glass
façade of a financial institution on
Westmoreland Street can be seen
the houses erected in the early
19th century by the Wide Street
Commissioners (above). Similarly,
from across the river, the dome of
Dublin's 18th-century Custom House
is reflected in a newly-completed
office development (opposite above).
The demands of pedestrian traffic have

also greatly changed of late. When the Ha'penny Bridge (far left) was first constructed over the Liffey in 1816, the river itself was still crowded with boats and the greatest hazard a walker faced was from horse-drawn carriages. Today cars pose a more serious danger, which is why Trinity College recently built this covered footbridge (near left) to bring students from one section of the campus to the other.

A fitting symbol for the new Dublin: the riverside civic offices from where the city's manager and his staff conduct the business of guiding Ireland's capital into the future. These buildings were themselves the subject of controversy, being erected over the site of 10th-century Viking ruins.

The same increase has occurred in the number of the bars, cafés and restaurants that have opened. There has been a remarkable proliferation of establishments available to discerning customers, as well as a startling rise in culinary standards.

The very public nature of coffee consumption in the new cafés – taken at a little table set up on the street – has also had an effect on Dublin's bars. Traditionally, these were designed to permit as little contact with the outside world as possible, so that drinkers could enjoy themselves in private. But a large number of the new wave of pubs and bars abandoned this design for a more overt expression of their function. Small windows were jettisoned in favour of large sheets of plate-glass, which not only allowed much more light into the interior but also made the latter more accessible to the outside world.

Retailing is another aspect of the city's commercial life that has altered radically of late. Again, very few of Dublin's long-established outlets have managed to survive the era of change. On the capital's principal shopping thoroughfare, Grafton Street, barely half a dozen premises have pedigrees dating back more than a decade, although several – Weir's the jewellers, the tobacconist James J. Fox and the furrier Barnardo's – have occupied their present sites since the 19th century. But during the 1990s, overseas retailers saw Dublin as a market in which to expand and took over premises until then often occupied by long-established family businesses. The reason for this interest was that the Irish economy, after well over a century of stagnation at best or decline at worst, had boomed with extraordinary rapidity. Indeed, a country which had been hopelessly backward in comparison with European neighbours, discovered it had the fastest growing economy among them, with annual growth rates of up to ten per cent. In the second half of the 1990s, the number of people at work in Ireland rose by more than thirty per cent, while during the same decade, the unemployment dropped from around twenty to less than four per cent of the population.

As so often in Dublin today, the modern and the ancient have become close neighbours. One of the blocks occupied by Dublin City Council stands directly in front of Christ Church Cathedral (above). The latter was founded in 1038 but, like so much else in the city, has undergone considerable changes in the intervening period. These still await the Council's offices which were only completed in the late 1990s.

Nearby in Temple Bar's Meeting House Square, the Gallery of Photography (left) is one of many new arts venues in the city. Others in the immediate vicinity include the National Photographic Archive and a children's cultural centre called the Ark. During the summer months the square hosts free open-air screenings of films.

Since the late 1980s, the eastern quays of Dublin have been transformed by the construction of new offices, primarily for the International Financial Services Centre (above), where more than 6,500 people are employed by a wide variety of global corporations.

The skyline of central Dublin (right) has scarcely changed for more than two hundred years, apart from the addition in the 1960s of Liberty Hall to on the north of the River Liffey and O'Connell Bridge House on the south. But demands for more inner-city accommodation is likely to mean this skyline will alter dramatically in the years ahead.

CONTEMPORARY
COMFORT

During the 1990s, more and more Dublin residents rediscovered the pleasures of living in the city: the ease of movement between their homes and their places of work; the convenience of having a wide variety of metropolitan facilities – galleries, theatres, cinemas – within immediate reach; the sense of playing a part in the rejuvenation of Ireland's capital. To meet the demand for inner-city living, imaginative schemes were devised for the transformation of old warehouses and commercial buildings.

Spread over two floors in a former clothing factory, Caroline Kennedy's apartment is a typical example of the accommodation recently created in Dublin using the city's old building stock.

Kennedy's guest bedroom displays her imaginative approach to interior decoration (left). The large carved cupboard came from Hong Kong while the painting hung nearby was bought in Rome. The porcelain bowl (above) on the other hand, is Irish and was made as a unique commission to mark the new millennium.

The relative poverty and lack of industrial development in Dublin during the 19th century means that the city has a smaller stock of former warehouses and factories than is found in other European capitals, where these have often been transformed into smart housing. Nevertheless, some such buildings today serve very different purposes from those originally intended. A former electricity warehouse, for example, is now a smart apartment block, as are the surviving section of a Victorian prison and an old whiskey distillery.

In 2000 Caroline Kennedy moved into her present home, a duplex apartment created in the upper storeys of what was once a 1940s clothing factory. The warehouse lies on the outskirts of the Liberties, one of the oldest districts of Dublin dating back to the Middle Ages, and in the 17th and 18th centuries, the centre of the city's silk-weaving trade. All around is evidence of this long-vanished prosperity, as well as the decay that followed and which is only now being decisively overcome. On nearby Clanbrassil Street, new housing has replaced the ramshackle buildings that used to serve as shops, selling what were described as antiques, but more often bric-a-brac and second-hand junk.

Kennedy is an extremely contented resident of the area. Founder of one of Ireland's most successful public relations companies, boasting a wide range of national and international clients, she has always lived in central Dublin since moving to the city from her native town of Thurles in County Tipperary some twenty years ago. 'I actually enjoy the anonymity of inner-city life,' she says. 'I like the broad social mix that you get here, with students and newly-arrived immigrants and families who have been living on the same streets for generations.'

With her office in another building, which also once served as a factory, Kennedy is clearly a fan not just of inner-city living, but also of urban renewal. The distance between home and work is no more than a ten-minute walk. 'It's the ease of access that I really appreciate,' she comments. 'This part of Dublin is its heart and soul and that engages me both professionally

The open-plan design of Caroline Kennedy's duplex apartment allows her to create spaces such as the dining area (left). 'Red is my favourite colour,' she says, which is why it is found throughout her home. The painting of a woman is by the French artist Claude Flach and was bought in St Tropez.

The three heads above the sofa in the living room on the upper floor (overleaf) are by John Boyd who lives in Dublin; they came from a gallery close to Kennedy's home. The embroidered cushions, on the other hand, were brought back from New Delhi while the large coffee table is Chinese.

and in my social life. The other advantage is that living here I'm the same distance from Brown Thomas (Dublin's most prestigious department store) on Grafton Street and the fruit and vegetable stalls on Camden Street.'

Spread over two floors and approximately twice the size of the average house in Dublin, Kennedy's apartment benefits from spectacular views across the city that she now calls home. From a garden balcony on the upper level, she enjoys views of Dublin's two cathedrals and far beyond. Inside, the rooms have high ceilings and floors covered in wooden parquet rescued from the old clothing factory during its restoration.

'To me, this particular style of living is akin to being in a New York loft,' observes Kennedy. 'Because of the full-length windows, there's lots of natural light and a real sense of airiness.' The design of her home allows Kennedy, a popular hostess, to give both small dinners and big parties for her many friends.

Among the consequences of the boom was the rediscovery of the merits of urban living. Ever since the 1800 Act of Union, there had been a flight by the more affluent sections of the population from the city centre to the suburbs and the capital suffered as its resident population steadily declined. That decline was decisively reversed in the 1990s.

Dubliners who leave their native city, even for just six months, are astonished at the changes that have taken place during their absence. And there are many more to come in the years ahead because this process of transformation has acquired its own momentum. One specific change that can be expected is a fundamental alteration of the city skyline. Unlike most cities developed during the 20th century, Dublin remained a low-rise place, spreading out rather than up. Liberty Hall, the capital's first high-rise building erected in 1962, at sixteen storeys still remains her tallest. But that cannot remain the case for much longer.

This is a thrilling time to live in Ireland's capital and to witness the speed and extent of the change taking place there. Unlike many old cities in Europe which have had their shape and character decisively fixed already, Dublin is in the throes of transformation, shedding her long-standing image of a dirty, neglected but beloved city which has been celebrated by so many writers over the past three centuries. There have been mistakes made and losses belatedly realized, but these must be accepted as an inevitable part of mutation. At the moment, it is impossible to say what the eventual character of a new Dublin will be, her form still as unclear as it must have been during the 18th century when the city was last altered in such a fundamental fashion. The only constant is the River Liffey, the Anna Livia of legend, forever observing Dublin's progress while making its own way through her centre.

Temple Bar is one of the oldest districts of Dublin. Its name is derived from Sir William Temple who owned a house and garden there in the 17th century. More than two hundred years later, Temple Bar enjoyed a resurgence thanks to a government-sponsored urban renewal project.

One of the clearest manifestations of Dublin's changed character are the annual celebrations hosted by the city on Ireland's annual national holiday, St Patrick's Day. This used to be a dismal occasion marked by heavy rain, as the anniversary has the misfortune to fall in the middle of the wet month of March. But in the mid-1990s, the city authorities decided to transform the occasion from a dispiriting and poorly supported event into a major four-day festival. The saint himself

now barely features, crowded out
by such features as an extravagant
fireworks display over the River Liffey,
a fleadh (traditional Irish music and
dancing) and a parade viewed by some
half a million spectators lining its
route. Even the sun occasionally
deigns to shine.

CONTEMPORARY
PENTHOUSE

Central Dublin is full of unexpected, and often unknown, residences, their plain façades betraying little evidence of what lies inside. A dockside warehouse converted into a luxurious home, a former meat packing plant transformed into a studio and living accommodation for two artists or, as shown here, a sweet factory refurbished to provide several storeys of office space topped by a duplex penthouse.

The building stands at the highest point of Dublin, a hill replete with the city's history over the past thousand years. Diagonally opposite rises Christ Church Cathedral, founded in 1038, while immediately behind lies the great mass of Dublin Castle, begun some two centuries later. The apartment's two most immediate neighbours reflect that juxtaposition of form and function which remains such a constant feature of the city. Next door is the church of St Werburgh, largely rebuilt in the 1760s and preserving probably the finest Georgian ecclesiastical interior with a carved wooden gallery and exquisite stuccowork. In total contrast, facing it is Burdock's, the most famous fish-and-chip shop in Dublin, outside which on most evenings a queue of customers can be seen stretching down the street.

'It's extraordinary to live at this point where so much of the city's history has taken place,' remarks the penthouse's owner, adding 'I'm sure this was a lookout tower in the Viking days.' A Dublin-born entrepreneur, he runs a philanthropic enterprise from his home under the name of the Academy of Everything is Possible.

Works of art are stacked against the wall of the penthouse apartment's main living space. Among those most immediately visible are large photographs of Sarajevo children by Louis Jaimes, a Keith Haring drawing and an oil by American artist James Mathers.

The apartment is full of evidence of the organization's work, such as a series of large photographs taken by French artist Louis Jaime. Showing children affected by war in Sarajevo, under the auspices of the Academy, some thirty of these were displayed on the walls of buildings around Dublin in 1997 in order to increase Irish awareness of the humanitarian disaster taking place in former Yugoslavia.

The apartment itself was only completed two years later but already seems full to the point of overflowing as its owner is an inveterate traveller, rarely remaining in Ireland, or anywhere else, for more than a few days. When he first bought the building in the early 1990s, this area of Dublin was very dilapidated and its resident population had been in steady decline for several decades. Since then, inner-city living has regained its popularity; several new apartment blocks have been constructed within close proximity of this penthouse and more are planned, while around the corner the Civic Trust has restored an 18th century merchant's house.

The penthouse itself is resolutely contemporary. A vast corner window juts out over the roadway below and offers stunning views of Christ Church Cathedral and the sun setting across the river behind the Phoenix Park. Spacious seating around the window and a specially commissioned oak table in front of it make this a natural gathering place whenever there are visitors. Natural materials have been used as much as possible both inside and out, because one of the apartment's finest features are its two gardens, the upper one filled with tubs of bamboo. From here the whole of Dublin beckons; north and south, east and west, it all looks tantalizingly close.

Within the penthouse, most rooms flow naturally into each other. So on the upper level an open-plan kitchen and dining area runs into the library as well as onto the bamboo roof garden. The apartment's only private quarters are two bedrooms and bathrooms and a steamroom/sauna.

Davy Byrne's (left) is one of the most famous pubs in Dublin; here during the course of his parambulations around the city in Ulysses, Leopold Bloom paused for a gorgonzola sandwich and a glass of burgundy. Regular fare at the beginning of the 20th century, but it is unlikely that either Bloom or his creator would recognise much on today's menu in Davy Byrne's. Indeed, the pub's interior would also surprise Joyce because, like so many other premises in Dublin, it has been transformed over the intervening period. What would the writer have made of the Morrison Hotel (right), one of a new class of establishments built during the boom of the 1990s? The exterior of glass overlooking the River Liffey gives way to lofty interiors decorated by one of the city's most famous designers John Rocha. In design and spirit, it is as far away as imaginable from the Dublin of James Joyce and Leopold Bloom.

By the early 1990s, barely a handful of long-established hotels remained in Dublin. However, one of the earliest signs of change came in 1993 when the Clarence Hotel – which, incidentally, stands on the site of the old Custom House on Wellington Quay – was purchased by two members of the band U2 and a Dublin businessman, Harry Crosbie. This triumvirate went to considerable trouble to restore the mid-19th century building and enhance its Arts and Crafts interiors, while upgrading all the guest facilities (above and right). Previously, the Clarence Hotel's clientele had been predominantly country clergy visiting Dublin and jurors who were brought to lunch there from the Four Courts across the river. Now its guests are more likely to be affluent and style-conscious members of the international business community and, thanks to the U2 connection, rock and pop musicians passing through Dublin.

CONTEMPORARY
LIGHT

If there is one characteristic shared by Dubliners it must be the desire for natural light in a city that for much of the year enjoys too little of this commodity. Hence the preference for large windows and pale-coloured interiors among many of the city's residents as they seek to maximize the daylight available, particularly during the grey winter months when Ireland is subjected to so much rainfall.

Botanical artist Patricia Jorgensen has had a variety of careers and homes, all of them reflected in the converted mews house where she has lived for twenty years. It sits on a laneway behind the much bigger property in central Dublin that was also once her home. When she chose to move to the mews, it was in semi-derelict condition, but had the advantage of being untouched by previous conversion. 'Because it had never been a house,' she explains, 'there was this great open room where the loose boxes and carriages had been kept. I changed virtually nothing. It's a very good flexible space and that's the key to its success.' She deliberately retained the high ground-floor area and filled it with light by turning the enormous carriage arch into a window. The only major structural alteration that she made inside the building was to install a pair of French windows at the front. These open into a conservatory which, in turn, looks out over a plant-filled courtyard; it serves as an occasional dining area during the summer.

A window in the main dining space looks onto the garden that Patricia Jorgensen has created behind the

Light is found in abundance throughout Patricia Jorgensen's converted mews home and nowhere more so than in her living room, where flowers and plants are found both on the tables and on the walls. The carpet here was made by V'soske Joyce to Patricia Jorgensen's own designs.

mews. Once a patch of wasteground, it is now filled with ferns, camellias and old-fashioned climbing roses. Because she entertains so often, her kitchen is extremely practical. The glass-fronted cabinets originally came from the butler's pantry in another house and the work surfaces and made from slabs of teak, which can be taken out and scrubbed down.

The upper floor is reached via a wooden spiral staircase in the centre of the main room. 'It doesn't take up nearly as much space as a regular set of stairs would in most houses,' she points out. 'It just flows upwards and allows air and light to circulate around it.' The balcony above provides access to the main bedroom, bathroom and Patricia Jorgensen's studio.

In the last of these, she works on the botanical paintings that have given so much pleasure both to herself and her admirers over the past decade. But she began her professional life working in another field, having studied fine art at college in her native Dublin. After graduating, she was employed by a Swedish textile printing firm in Galway as a technical artist. While in the west of Ireland, she also began working with a newly established weaving company called V'soske Joyce which continues to produce her designs for clients. Moving back to Dublin, she married a Danish-born couturier, Ib Jorgensen, with whom she afterwards worked, producing designs for his evening wear, which could be appliquéd, hand-painted, beaded and embroidered.

By the late 1970s, Patricia Jorgensen had begun exhibiting her own artwork, but it was only following her divorce and move to the mews house that the opportunity to concentrate on painting became possible. Having grown up with two old gardens – those owned by her parents and her grandmother – and then created her own, she became increasingly drawn to botanical art. 'I went back to flowers and plants in a gradual way. I started by drawing, mostly doing still-lifes and then there were lots of fabrics in my paintings. But gradually everything else gave way and the flowers remained.'

Through the wooden spiral staircase, which was inserted into the mews house to interrupt the internal space as little as possible, some of Patricia Jorgensen's botanical paintings can be seen hanging on the walls (left). In winter, the solid-fuel stove keeps the entire living-room area comfortably warm.

The artist's studio is at the top of the stairs in a room overlooking her own inspirational garden (above). Treating her work as a form of portraiture, she says, 'In a good portrait the sitter's pose or posture reveals character. So it is for me with flower painting. And just as the face is the lively culmination of the body, so its bloom or flower is the face of the plant.'

There were a number of friends ready to offer assistance including Susana, Lady Walton, widow of the English composer Sir William Walton. Over five summers, she invited Patricia Jorgensen to spend several weeks painting in her garden, La Mortella, on the Italian island of Ischia. 'She was a wonderful patron,' the artist comments, 'acquiring almost all my gardenscapes and flower studies, which she used to illustrate her first garden book.' Patricia Jorgensen has since gone on to chronicle a number of other important gardens both in Ireland and overseas.

Working at La Mortella also confirmed the artist's own preferences. 'I particularly like tropical, rather lush plants,' she says. 'The thing I definitely don't paint are tiny miniature plants: I'm a painter rather than an illustrator. I do like to allow the paint to speak, to be a valid part of the work rather than be subservient to it. Many of the larger-scale plants lend themselves better to the way I work.'

Patricia Jorgensen insists that she is not a traditional botanical painter, producing pictures that are primarily diagrammatic and scientific. Instead, she argues, her approach is closer to that of a portraitist. 'I want to capture the life, character and personality of plants in a decorative design while still maintaining botanical accuracy. For example, I see the trunk of a tree or the stem of a flower as the equivalent of the spine in the human body. Just as the spine determines posture in our body, so the 'posture' of a plant is determined by its stem.'

Painting plants and flowers has now become her constant occupation. 'It's wonderful because I love the work and it has provided me with an entree into all kinds of fascinating gardens.'

Patricia Jorgensen can seat up to twenty-four guests for dinner, but prefers smaller gatherings around her Regency dining table, behind which are displayed the artist's collection of antique jelly moulds. On the wall to the left hangs a tapestry made to her own design.

'A lot done, more to do', ran the slogan for a political party during the Irish general election of 2002. The same sentence could be applied to Dublin, which has seen its appearance and character improve enormously since the early 1990s. Much of the city now exudes an air of metropolitan prosperity, as embodied by the popular Unicorn restaurant (above), where politicians, journalists and pundits meet for lunch on Saturday. A bar called Zanzibar on Dublin's quays (right) is also representative of the city's new-found confidence and sophistication. Elsewhere, evidence is easily found of what many parts of the capital looked like before its economic boom. Only Butt Bridge (right) separates a gleaming glass office development, taller than any other in the centre of Dublin, from an old-fashioned pub and a derelict site, which still awaits an improvement to its fortunes.

'Everyone comments on the sense of tranquility here,' says Helen Roycroft of the house she shares with Peter Sweeney. Completed in 1998, the two-storey building in an area of Dublin, almost entirely covered in 19th-century terraced homes, won a prize for its design from the Architectural Association of Ireland. The interior was left as simple as possible. Even the kitchen area appears to dissolve into the wall behind, thanks to the consistent use of plain white for all the units.

CONTEMPORARY
MINIMAL

Conservatism is a consistent trait of the Irish character, but occasionally this trend is bucked. So musicians Peter Sweeney and Helen Roycroft commissioned award-winning Dublin architectural practice McCullough Mulvin to design a new home on the site of a former mews house. The result was a property strikingly different from its neighbours, yet at ease in the environment. One of its most immediate and abiding features is the serenity that it exudes.

On a floor of waxed white maple
which runs the full fifteen metres of
the house's open-plan first floor, sits
a refectory table in maple and ebony
made for the room by Irish furniture
designer Stephen O'Briain (above).
Other items commissioned within
Ireland for the house include furniture
by the Dublin-based company
Duff Tisdall and a rug woven by
Stephanie Conroy.

Although windows cover much of
the rear of the house, it still enjoys
considerable privacy thanks to the
strategic use of acid-etched glass, as
well as careful planting in the garden
by Helen Conroy (right). And despite
the relatively small size of the site on
which it was built, there is still space
inside for a music room where
Peter Sweeney can practise his
organ playing (opposite).

DUBLIN VISITORS' GUIDE

As local residents will confirm, Dublin is a city in transition. From being a quiet place in which nothing appeared to change, it has become a city of constant change. Any guide to its services therefore runs the risk of rapidly becoming outdated: restaurants which were au courant one season, may be closed the next; shops open and close with bewildering speed; and what was fashionable last year is likely to have since fallen from favour.

The speed of change experienced by the city means that scarcely any of its older establishments have survived and their number continues to dwindle. Typically, until the mid-1990s, there used to be a premises on Parliament Street which had sold swords and cutlery since the 18th century; it has since been taken over as part of yet another pub. This story is repeated across the city, so that scarcely any businesses with a history longer than a decade can be discovered.

Depending on your outlook, you will find this process of persistent mutation either dispiriting or exhilarating. The latter is certainly the better response, but it does mean that visitors to Dublin should not expect to be discovering lots of charming, old-fashioned locations seemingly untouched by the passage of time. What they are far more likely to encounter are places so newly opened that the paint on the walls has scarcely had time to dry, and where even the

members of staff are not altogether sure what is on offer. Yes, there are still a few spots which have, at least so far, escaped redevelopment and they are included here. But by far the greater part of the places mentioned are relatively new and in this respect they offer an accurate picture of contemporary living in Dublin.

CALENDAR OF KEY EVENTS AND PUBLIC HOLIDAYS

1 January: New Year's Day
February–March: Six Nations Rugby Tournament at Lansdowne Road stadium
17 March: St Patrick's Day
Good Friday: Public Holiday
Easter Monday: Public Holiday
Late April: Four-day Irish National Hunt Festival at Punchestown racecourse
First Mondays in May, June and August: Public Holidays
May bank holiday weekend: Heineken Green Energy rock festival
16 June: Bloomsday
Last Sunday in June: Irish Derby Day at the Curragh
First weekend in August: Witness rock festival at Fairyhouse racecourse
August: All-Ireland hurling and Gaelic football matches in Croke Park (finals held in second half of September)
Third week in August: Kerrygold Horse Show
Mid–late September: Dublin Jazz Festival
Early October: Dublin Theatre Festival
Monday nearest 31 October: Public Holiday
25 and 26 December: Public Holidays
26 to 28 December: Leopardstown Racecourse Festival

HOTELS

FOUR SEASONS HOTEL DUBLIN
Simmonscourt Road, Dublin 4
Tel: 01 6654000
Fax: 01 6654099
Web: www.fourseasons.com
A purpose-built hotel which opened in Dublin's most prestigious suburb in the spring of 2001, the Four Seasons is not an object of beauty, either internally or externally. However, any visual

failings are sufficiently compensated for by the attentiveness of the staff and the great comfort of the facilities, as well as truly excellent food in the main restaurant.

THE WESTIN
College Green, Dublin 2
Tel: 01 6451000
Fax: 01 6451234
Web: www.westin.com
Impossible to stay more centrally than this, unless inside the grounds of Trinity College, the Westin's nearest neighbour. Opened in autumn 2001, the premises incorporates two 19th-century banking halls, one of which now serves as a splendid ballroom. The building's other notable feature is the four-storied, glass-topped atrium. Because of the quirky nature of the site, all the bedrooms are different from each other.

LE MERIDIEN SHELBOURNE
27 St Stephen's Green, Dublin 2
Tel: 01 6634500
Fax: 01 6616006
Web: www.lemeridien-shelbourne.com
Dublin's oldest hotel, the Shelbourne dates back to 1824 and has frequently been mentioned by Irish writers. Elizabeth Bowen even wrote a history of the place. It is now part of the Meridien chain, which tends to give some of its services a global blandness. But Dubliners still flock to the Shelbourne thanks to its great location and its intensely sociable public areas, especially the Horseshoe Bar which on Friday evenings tends to be so packed with people that they spill out into the main hall. A good spot to watch the locals at play.

THE MERRION HOTEL
21–24 Upper Merrion Street, Dublin 2
Tel: 01 6030600
Fax: 01 6030700
Web: www.merrionhotel.com

Although only a few years old, the Merrion appears to have been around forever, helped by the fact that its front block was created from four 18th-century aristocratic townhouses (one of them the birthplace of the Duke of Wellington). Some of the interiors are exquisite, the ceilings decorated with elaborate rococo plasterwork, while the main public rooms hold an important collection of old Irish furniture and paintings. Weather permitting, it is possible to drink and dine in the rear gardens, but given the country's climate, a wiser alternative might be the inviting bar created from the houses' former cellars.

THE FITZWILLIAM HOTEL
St Stephen's Green, Dublin 2
Tel: 01 4787000
Fax: 01 4787878
Web: www.fitzwilliamhotel.com
Ever since it opened, the Fitzwilliam has striven to be more fashionable than has yet been the case. But really, this hotel does not need to make such an effort because, thanks in part to its interiors designed by Sir Terence Conran and his team, it has an inherently cool but comfortable character. Minimalist in style, the rooms are lavishly fitted out with marble, leather and dark woods. The main restaurant has recently been taken over by one of Dublin's most distinguished chefs, Kevin Thornton, making this one of the best dining spots in the city.

THE CLARENCE
6–8 Wellington Quay, Dublin 2
Tel: 01 4070800
Fax: 01 4070820
Web: www.theclarence.ie
Until the early 1990s, the Clarence was a quiet hotel, much frequented by priests visiting Dublin from their country parishes. Then it was bought as a consortium (which included two members of U2) and given such a thorough overhaul that clerics are unlikely to be seen on the premises again. The original arts-and-crafts inspired interior remains,

but has been considerably smartened up. The in-house restaurant, the Tea Room, serves delicious food in quietly beautiful surroundings, while at weekends, the Octagon Bar is popular with young, smart drinkers.

HERBERT PARK HOTEL
Ballsbridge Terrace, Dublin 4
Tel: 01 6672200
Fax: 01 6672595
Web: www.herbertparkhotel.ie
Located next to one of the city's prettiest parks and in the midst of its most affluent suburb, the Herbert Park is quietly luxurious and unfussy. The main lobby, bar and restaurant all benefit from an abundance of natural light and staff who pay constant attention to guests' needs. An ideal location for visitors who wish to be relatively close to the centre, but sufficiently removed from its bustle.

THE MORRISON HOTEL
Ormond Quay, Dublin 1
Tel: 01 8872400
Fax: 01 8744039
Web: www.morrisonhotel.ie
For nearly two centuries, the northside of Dublin has never been as fashionable as its southside. The Morrison, which opened in the late 1990s, was determined to reverse this trend and has enjoyed some success in the smart crowd that it attracts. The draw is the hotel's very stylish interior, its decoration overseen by fashion designer John Rocha using an abundance of large gilt mirrors and velvet sofas. The Halo restaurant is a room every bit as gorgeous as the food served there, while the basement Lobo bar and club are worth visiting, if only briefly.

THE CLARION HOTEL
International Financial Services Centre, Dublin 1
Tel: 01 4338800
Fax: 01 4338811
Web: www.clarionhotelifsc.com

Overlooking the River Liffey and in the centre of Dublin's new financial district, the Clarion's clientele is primarily drawn from the business community. But that ought not to deter other visitors, as the place is stylish and airy, with smartly designed contemporary spaces, such as the bar serving Thai food. For those exhausted from negotiating deals, there is also a superb basement gym, complete with 18-metre swimming pool.

THE MORGAN
10 Fleet Street, Dublin 2
Tel: 01 6793939
Fax: 01 6793946
Web: www.themorgan.com
The Morgan is as close as Dublin gets to that international phenomenon, the boutique hotel. Its convenient location in the fashionable and crowded Temple Bar area is a plus for younger guests, but may not suit more mature visitors looking for somewhere quiet. While the bedrooms are wonderfully finished and fitted – everything from Egyptian cotton linen to ISDN connections – the Morgan does not have an in-house restaurant and its bar tends to get very busy.

BUSWELLS HOTEL
23–27 Molesworth Street, Dublin 2
Tel: 01 6146500
Fax: 01 6762090
Web: wwwquinnhotels.com
Although its reception rooms have been thoroughly refurbished of late, Buswells has preserved its character as a wonderfully comfortable and old-fashioned hotel, of the kind that has all but disappeared from Dublin. Contained within a series of 18th-century houses, the place remains relaxed despite its nearest neighbour being the state's parliament; expect to meet lots of politicians and pundits in the bar.

THE SCHOOLHOUSE HOTEL
2-8 Northumberland Road, Dublin 4
Tel: 01 6675014
Fax: 01 6675015
For somewhere a little different in Dublin, the School House is recommended. As the name makes clear, this delightful red-brick Gothic building is a former school, originally built in 1860. Despite its conversion to a hotel, many of the original features have been retained and the décor is traditional throughout, with the added bonus of modern conveniences. It also boasts a fine location, next to a particularly scenic stretch of the Grand Canal, but just ten minutes walk from the city centre.

RESTAURANTS

BANG CAFE
11 Merrion Row, Dublin 2
Tel: 01 6760898
Living up to its name, this ultra-fashionable eatery was opened by the twin Stokes brothers and caters primarily to their own young, good-looking and affluent crowd. Not necessarily the best choice for an intimate dinner, Bang is invariably noisy

and crowded. It offers a diverse menu ranging from baked Thai seabass to the house special: jumbo bangers and mash.

CHAPTER ONE
18–19 Parnell Square, Dublin 1
Tel: 01 8732266
This part of the north city is not well provided with decent places to eat, which is why Chapter One – located in the basement of the Dublin Writers' Museum, hence its name – has enjoyed such steady success. That and its excellent food, of course. The restaurant is conveniently close to a number of important cultural venues including the Hugh Lane Gallery and the Gate Theatre. Members of the latter's audience often eat here either before or after performances.

THE COMMONS
Newman House, 85–86 St Stephen's Green, Dublin 2
Tel: 01 4780530
James Joyce ate here as an undergraduate, in the days when this building was part of Dublin's University College. However, the food he would have been offered in the basement of one of the city's loveliest 18th-century houses was probably not nearly as delicious as that offered to guests today. Chef Aiden Byrne regularly wins awards for his cooking, essentially classic in character with contemporary flourishes. For a lighter version of the same, the Commons Cafe operates out of the National Concert Hall on nearby Earlsfort Terrace.

EDEN
Meeting House Square, Dublin 2
Tel: 01 6705372
When it opened in 1996, Eden was the most sought-after restaurant in town, with waiting lists weeks long. That time has thankfully passed, but not the culinary standards that made the place so very popular. Contemporary cooking is offered in contemporary surroundings. One wall of glass overlooks a pedestrian square where free cultural events are often staged. Weather permitting, a table outdoors can be a bonus for anyone who enjoys people-watching.

ELY
22 Ely Place, Dublin 2
Tel: 01 6768986
Ely is probably unique in Dublin, being a wine bar with a first-class cellar, delicious food and elegant surroundings. Occupying a couple of floors in a Georgian house, it provides wine by the glass or the bottle and a small menu of fresh food to accompany your drink. The clientele tends to be quite young, but this should not deter anyone as mature as some of the vintages on offer.

LA STAMPA
35 Dawson Street, Dublin 2
Tel: 01 6778611
It may have an Italian name – and even an occasional Italian presence on the menu – but La Stampa has the appearance and character of a classic French

brasserie. Possibly the biggest, and certainly the most opulent, dining room in Dublin, the atmosphere here is always celebratory, as though the good times could never end. First-rate food and fantastic surroundings make La Stampa a consistent favourite.

L'ECRIVAIN
109a Baggot Street Lower, Dublin 2
Tel: 01 6611919
With chef Derry Clarke in the kitchen and his wife Sallyanne looking after guests in the dining room, L'Ecrivain is deservedly successful. Dublin's many celebrated writers are acknowledged in the restaurant's name and on its walls, but the main emphasis is on food rather than literature. Early booking is recommended if you want to sample some of the best of modern Irish cuisine.

LOCKS
1 Windsor Terrace, Portobello, Dublin 8
Tel: 01 4543391
A pretty little house overlooking a leafy stretch of the Grand Canal, Locks provides classic French cooking with just a hint of the Hibernian added to the pot. Long-time proprietor Claire Douglas is a constant presence on the premises and this ensures that standards remain high. One of the best places to go for an undisturbed dinner *à deux*.

THE MERMAID CAFE
69–70 Dame Street, Dublin 2
Tel: 01 6708236
Located on one of the city's busiest thoroughfares and next to one of its main theatres, the Mermaid is a very public place to dine, not least thanks to its extensive windows. No chance of privacy here, therefore, but plenty of opportunity for relaxed, delicious food, such as spicy crabcakes and the enormous seafood platter. The proprietors have opened take-away premises next door, amusingly called Gruel. Thankfully, this name does not reflect what is for sale.

ONE PICO
5–6 Molesworth Place, Dublin 2
Tel: 01 6760300
In an old mews building, tucked down a laneway, One Pico is worth discovering thanks to the cooking of chef/proprietor Eamonn O'Reilly. His approach can best be summarized as contemporary Irish, a clever mix of the familiar and the unexpected but always delicious, served in a comfortable discreet room by attentive staff.

RESTAURANT PATRICK GUILBAUD
Merrion Hotel, 21 Upper Merrion Street, Dublin 2
Tel: 01 6764192
Frenchman Patrick Guilbaud takes his food very seriously and so do his clients. This restaurant was the first in modern times to propose high culinary standards to Dubliners and it continues to set the pace for more recent arrivals in the city. Within walls covered with fine paintings by the likes of William Scott, the setting and service are impeccable and serious, if not sometimes reverential. Expect delicious gallic food but at a price.

ROLY'S BISTRO
7 Ballsbridge Terrace, Dublin 4
Tel: 01 6682611
Although the eponymous Roly Saul has long-since departed – he now runs a rather smart brasserie bearing his name in the coastal suburb of Dun Laoghaire – this Ballsbridge bistro remains as popular as ever, thanks to the abiding presence of chef Colin O'Daly. The surroundings are inviting, the menu full of familiar treats, like confit of duck and Irish stew, the bill never too shockingly high; no wonder the place has such a loyal clientele.

THE TEA ROOM
Clarence Hotel, 6–8 Wellington Quay, Dublin 2
Tel: 01 4070813
A spacious, elegant, wood-panelled interior, the Tea Room has to be one of the most pleasant places in which to eat in Dublin. And the food is first-rate as well, supervised by chef Antony Ely. The menu's culinary inspiration is diverse but standards remain consistently high. The hotel's connection with U2 means that visiting celebrities often dine here.

THORNTON'S
Fitzwilliam Hotel, St Stephen's Green, Dublin 2
Tel: 01 4787008
Quietly working in his own premises during the 1990s, Kevin Thornton became perhaps the most admired chef in Dublin. In September 2002 he took over the main restaurant of the Fitzwilliam Hotel but otherwise changed little in his approach to cooking. Standards are very high, and so too are the prices.

THE TROCADERO
3 St Andrew's Street, Dublin 2
Tel: 01 6799772
Both the décor and menu of the Trocadero appear to have remained unaltered for the past thirty years and yet the crowds still pour through its narrow entrance. There are several reasons for this, the most important being the presence of long-time manager Robert Doggett who soothes, cajoles and charms everyone without favour. The abundance of signed photographs covering the walls testify to the Trocadero's popularity among actors, large numbers of whom eat here after the theatres have closed for the night.

THE UNICORN
12b Merrion Court, Merrion Row, Dublin 2
Tel: 01 6762182
No one would ever think of going to the Unicorn for the food, even though this has improved immeasurably in recent years. A long-established Italian restaurant, its primary attraction is as the favourite meeting place for many of Dublin's most animated conversationalists, chatterers and gossips. Friday and Saturday lunchtimes are especially popular and it is in this restaurant that some of the city's most entertaining scandals and stories were first told.

CAFÉS

BEWLEY'S ORIENTAL CAFÉ
78 Grafton Street, Dublin 2
Tel: 01 6776761
A Dublin institution since the 19th century, Bewley's has undergone many changes over the intervening period while retaining the loyal affection of locals. Perhaps uniquely, it also continues to transcend all social, economic and generational differences; everyone visits Bewley's. The main room here is decorated with wonderful stained glass by the Irish artist Harry Clarke. While full meals are available, the best treat remains a cup of coffee and a classic sticky bun.

BUTLER'S CHOCOLATE CAFE
24 Wicklow Street, Dublin 2
Tel: 01 6710591
It's raining yet again (this is Dublin, after all), you're cold, wet and in need of a treat. What better, therefore, than to slip into a seat here and order a delicious mug of hot chocolate. Other beverages are also available, of course, along with the company's scrumptious handmade chocolates.

COBALT CAFÉ
16 North Great George's Street, Dublin 1
Tel: 01 8730313
On one of the grandest of the city's Georgian streets, this café occupies the ground-floor rooms of a house serving tea, coffee and light meals at lunchtime. The walls are covered with artwork which customers can buy.

THE EPICUREAN FOOD HALL
46 Middle Abbey Street and 13–14 Upper Liffey Street, Dublin 1
No telephone
This part of central north Dublin is entirely devoted to retail premises, so there is no reason why visitors to the city would necessarily find themselves there. But the Epicurean Food Hall is worth a detour; a dozen-odd independent outlets brought together and offering a wide range of cuisine ranging from Turkish to Japanese to Irish. There is some seating, but never enough for the crowds that throng here during the peak lunch period. The perfect place to find everything necessary for a gourmet picnic.

LA MAISON DES GOURMETS
15 Castle Market, Dublin 2
Tel: 01 6727258
The name says it all; this is the spot for all food lovers as the extensive range of French breads, cakes and pastries are all baked and for sale on the premises. Upstairs is a little café, barely seating more than 20 people at a time, where the fresh produce can be eaten, accompanied by a discerning choice of teas and coffees.

QUEEN OF TARTS
City Hall, Dame Street, Dublin 2
Tel: 01 6722925
The City Hall is one of Dublin's examples of 18th-century neoclassical architecture, now meticulously restored and open to the public. In its former cellars are a fascinating exhibition devoted to the history of the city, and this little delight of a café where you can reward your cultural endeavours with home-made cakes and pastries.

THE WINDING STAIR CAFÉ
40 Lower Ormond Quay, Dublin 1
Tel: 01 8733292
On the premises of one of Dublin's finest second-hand bookshops, this café is a particular favourite with literate students, gaggles of whom can be found lingering over tables. The Winding Stair is a great place to find inexpensive but out-of-print Irish books. Here is an opportunity to browse the shelves and have a decent coffee at the same time.

PUBS AND BARS

THE BAILEY
2 Duke Street, Dublin 2
Tel: 01 6704939
A legendary Dublin pub with distinguished literary credentials, The Bailey has undergone several transformations in the past couple of decades and has now been reincarnated into a smart bar, which looks as though it belongs on the pages of a style magazine. However, although the décor may be global modern, the crowd is resolutely local.

THE BRAZEN HEAD
20 Lower Bridge Street, Dublin 8
Tel: 01 6795186
Reputably Dublin's oldest pub (it dates back to 1688), the Brazen Head suffers from being in one of the less salubrious parts of the city. However, the location never seems to deter overseas visitors, who come here probably in greater numbers than the resident population. Worth calling into if in the area.

LA CAVE
28 South Anne Street, Dublin 2
Tel: 01 6794409
A tiny basement wine bar that plays up its French associations with lots of francophile posters. La Cave does serve food, but that always seems of secondary importance. A good spot to visit should you grow tired of Irish pubs or need somewhere to go when they have closed – La Cave remains open until 2 am daily.

DAKOTA
8 South William Street, Dublin 2
Tel: 01 6727696
Despite its considerable size, this former warehouse converted into a bar can become excessively crowded and noisy during weekend nights. Better, therefore, to lounge on one of its capacious brown leather sofas during the day sampling from the wide range of house cocktails.

DAVY BYRNE'S
21 Duke Street, Dublin 2
Tel: 01 6775217
Definitely a Dublin institution, Davy Byrne's was immortalized by James Joyce in *Ulysses* as the place where Leopold Bloom had his gorgonzola sandwich and glass of burgundy. The décor has changed a bit since 1904 as it now includes 1950s murals, added by Dublin artist Harry Kernoff. But the service, drink and food are still excellent even if Bloom's choice of sandwich is not necessarily on the bill of fare.

THE DAWSON LOUNGE
25 Dawson Street, Dublin 2
Tel: 01 6775909
Said to be the smallest pub in the city, the Dawson Lounge is found in a basement at the bottom of a vertiginous flight of stairs. Understandably, it can have the air of a private club, but it's cosy and can be a welcome refuge from the cold streets outside. Of course, it is not for those who suffer from claustrophobia.

DOHENY & NESBITT
5 Lower Baggot Street, Dublin 2
Tel: 01 6762945
Like almost every other Dublin pub, Doheny & Nesbitt has been extended in recent years, but this has not adversely affected either the appearance or character of the original bar. Famous for being the haunt of politicians, lawyers, senior civil servants and journalists, during the afternoon it also tends to attract drinkers who have left long and liquid lunches in adjacent restaurants.

THE FRONT LOUNGE
33–34 Parliament Street, Dublin 2
Tel: 01 6704112
One of the best of the new breed of Dublin bars, the Front Lounge attracts a crowd as glamorous as its surroundings, the latter featuring lots of jewel-coloured velvet sofas and large plaster sculptures. Meanwhile, the crowd tends to be highly animated and intensely social, so this is not the best place for a quiet pint.

THE GLOBE
11 South Great George's Street, Dublin 2
Tel: 01 6711220
The Globe opened in 1993 when Irish bars were customarily dim and dingy. Its big plate-glass windows and airy interior furnished with wooden tables and benches was definitely different then, if much copied since. The pub remains highly popular, helped by good lunchtime food and the possibility of live jazz at the weekends.

GROGAN'S CASTLE LOUNGE
15 South William Street, Dublin 2
Tel: 01 6779320
Grogan's will never win any awards in the style stakes, but it resolutely remains unchanged by the economic boom that has taken place outside its doors. Instead, the pub seems quite unaltered since it was a haunt of Dublin writer Flann O'Brien in the 1950s and still draws the same eclectic crowd of artists, would-be artists and those who have chosen to put any art they may possess into their conversation.

THE HORSESHOE BAR
Shelbourne Hotel, St Stephen's Green, Dublin 2
Tel: 01 6766471
The Shelbourne Hotel has two bars, one large, the other small. The latter is the Horseshoe and, despite its diminutive size, can attract a substantial crowd, a mixture of people who run the country and others who merely think they do so. One of the best free shows in the city is to watch the behaviour of the Horseshoe's clientele, especially as the evening progresses and the effects of alcohol become apparent.

THE LONG HALL
51 South Great George's Street, Dublin 2
Tel: 01 4751590
The exterior promises little, the interior offers much. The Long Hall precisely lives up to its name: a long, narrow space which has the appearance of being unaltered for at least a century. The décor and accumulated bric-a-brac – including wonderful old mirrors – make drinking here a real pleasure.

MULLIGAN'S
8 Poolbeg Street, Dublin 2
Tel: 01 6775582
Hidden away on a decidedly unprepossessing backstreet, Mulligan's is another Dublin pub that deserves to be described as an institution. There may not be sawdust on the floor, but little has altered in the place's history. Expect little seating, and often not much by way of talking, but the chance to sample a serious pint of Guinness.

NEARY'S
1 Chatham Street, Dublin 2
Tel: 01 6778596
Identifiable by the handsome Victorian lamps decorating its exterior, Neary's is well known as a lunchtime meeting place where delicious plates of smoked or fresh salmon are available. A door at the back of the main bar opens onto a lane opposite the performers' entrance of the Gaiety Theatre, so actors often slip in here. For quieter times, try the little bar to the left of the entrance.

ODEON
57 Harcourt Street, Dublin 2
Tel: 01 4782088
Occupying what was once the main ticket office of a former railway station, Odeon seemingly can accommodate up to a thousand people and, on some nights, certainly gives the impression of doing so. To avoid the crowds and see this handsome space at its best, try Sunday afternoons for a leisurely brunch with the newspapers.

O'DONOGHUE'S
15 Merrion Row, Dublin 2
Tel: 01 6762807
Generations of Dubliners and visitors have packed into O'Donoghue's to catch live performaces of traditional Irish music. Some of the musicians have been famous, others are unknown. However, this venue remains probably the best and most convenient to hear what is being played all around the country.

THE PALACE
21 Fleet Street, Dublin 2
Tel: 01 6793037
An authentic example of the Victorian bar at its most enticing, the Palace is an essay in polished wood and etched glass. The cosiest place to sit is in the little snug at the back, but this can often be full, as the rest of the premises. It is traditionally a favourite among journalists, as the offices of *The Irish Times* newspaper are just a minute's walk away.

RYAN'S
28 Parkgate Street, Dublin 8
Tel: 01 6719352
The beauty of its Victorian interior and the convenience of its location, adjacent to the Phoenix Park, mean that Ryan's features on the majority of tourist trails. But locals drink there too, drawn as much by the quality of the stout as by the old mahogany and oak panelling, brass lamps and gilt mirrors. Bar food is available on the ground floor and more substantial fare on offer in the first-floor restaurant.

THE STAG'S HEAD
1 Dame Court, Dublin 2
Tel: 01 6793701
The Stag's Head dates back to the 18th century, but was rebuilt in 1895. Since then, little appears to have been altered. Secreted down a little backstreet, but nevertheless very central, the pub is one of those hidden gems that delight anyone lucky enough to find it and settle down for a drink at the long, marble-topped bar counter. The menu offers excellent bar food.

THOMAS READ
1–3 Parliament Street, Dublin 2
Tel: 01 6771487
First opened seven years ago, these premises look more like a continental café than a traditional Irish pub, not least thanks to the abundance of tables and chairs. Read's is comfortable and relaxed during the day, fairly busy at lunchtime – fine hearty fare on offer – and frequently so packed with customers in the evening that they can spill out onto the pavement. Timing your visit depends on what sort of experience you want.

SHOPPING:
FASHION AND ACCESSORIES

ALIAS TOM
2–5 Duke House, Grafton Street, Dublin 2
Tel: 01 6715443
Probably the best menswear store in Dublin, if not the country. Tom Kennedy's long-established premises carry a wide range of labels, most of which will be familiar to the international traveller such as Prada, Donna Karan and Issey Miyake.

A-WEAR
26 Grafton Street, Dublin 2
Tel: 01 6717200
The flagship store for a chain of Irish-owned outlets stocking inexpensive women's fashion.

Predominantly aimed at the younger end of the market, it is always worth checking what is in stock, as this changes almost weekly.

BROWN THOMAS
88–95 Grafton Street, Dublin 2
Tel: 01 6056666
Ireland's leading department store is a beautiful place to visit even if you do not intend to spend money there. As befits its status, the shop carries all the most important Irish and international names in women's and men's fashion, plus an abundance of household goods, giftware and, indeed, almost everything else that might be required.

BT2
28–29 Grafton Street, Dublin 2
Tel: 01 6056666
An offshoot of Brown Thomas, BT2 is aimed firmly at the youth market, both male and female, albeit those representatives of it who are fairly affluent. It is therefore crammed with the latest offerings from the likes of Ralph Lauren and Tommy Hilfiger.

CUBA
13 Trinity Street, Dublin 2
Tel: 01 6727489
Together with its sister shop Hobo on the opposite side of the same street, Cuba caters for young, fashion-conscious, but relatively impoverished consumers. New Irish designers such as Graham Cruz and Celestine Cooney can be discovered here, alongside some international names including Maharishi and Evisu.

COSTUME
10/11 Castle Market, Dublin 2
Tel: 01 6794188
Billie Tucker, whose family has been in the clothing manufacturing business for decades, opened this little shop in the late 1990s as an outlet for her own interest in fashion – look out for the likes of Anna Sui and London-based Irishman Pauric Sweeney – and for her daughter Leigh whose pretty, wearable designs are carried here.

THE DESIGN CENTRE
Powerscourt Townhouse Centre,
South William Street, Dublin 2
Tel: 01 6795718
In various incarnations, the Design Centre has been around for two decades as a place in which to discover new names in Irish fashion. It may not be as avant-garde as it once was, but it remains a great place to see what is being produced for the local market by such designers as Mariad Whisker and Lyn Mar.

DIFFUSION
47 Clontarf Road, Dublin 3
Tel: 01 8331592
In one of the more prosperous northside suburbs, owner Kate Gaffney has here created a jewel of a shop dedicated to the needs of her very devoted clientele. The labels tend to be diverse, but are

usually from international collections, including Mathew Williamson, Cerruti, Sophie Sitbon and Ally Capellino.

HAVANA
64 Donnybrook, Dublin 4
Tel: 01 2602707
A blend of local and overseas names is available here from experienced retailer Nikki Creedon. She usually stocks the Irish knitwear designer Lainey Keogh, plus Ann Demeulemeester, Yohji Yamamoto and Nicole Farhi; but every season introduces an element of surprise.

KHAN
1 Rock Hill, Blackrock, Co Dublin
Tel: 01 2781646
Deryn Mackey has worked hard to make sure she carries what her well-heeled customers want and provides it for them along with exceptionally attentive service. Among the familiar labels here are Philosophy di Alberta Ferretti and Elspeth Gibson.

LOUISE KENNEDY
56 Merrion Square, Dublin 2
Tel: 01 6620056
One of Ireland's most successful designers, Louise Kennedy has turned this 18th-century townhouse into an exquisite mini-department store. Of course it carries her own range of elegant clothing for women, plus the tableware she has created for Tipperary Crystal, but it also offers furniture and accessories by David Linley, hats by Philip Treacy along with a variety of other goods, all displayed in beautiful rooms.

PLATFORM
50 South William Street, Dublin 2
Tel: 01 6777380
Precisely the kind of quirky, individual shop that a capital city should have in abundance, but is all too rare in Dublin. A blend of cutting-edge Irish and international designers are brought together with flair by Joan Wood who always makes her selection look fresh and fascinating.

SMOCK
20–22 West Essex Street, Dublin 2
Tel: 01 6139000
Without doubt, the most interesting women's clothes shop in the Temple Bar area of the city at the moment. Smock carries a lot of Belgian designers such as Dries van Noten and Veronique Branquinho along with young Irish names including Jacob Tutu. Shoes, bags and a range of other accessories also stocked.

VIVIEN WALSH
24 Lower Stephen Street, Dublin 2
Tel: 01 4755031
Probably now Ireland's most successful costume jewelry designer, Vivien Walsh produces a new collection of work every season. This is stocked in her shop alongside a constantly changing array of women's clothing and accessories which she has

collected on her travels. The shop is slightly off the beaten track but worth seeking out.

ANTIQUES AND
SECOND-HAND GOODS

CATHACH BOOKS
10 Duke Street, Dublin 2
Tel: 01 6718676
Looking for a first edition of a book by Joyce or Beckett? Then this is the place to come, but be prepared to pay a high price. Cathach Books only carries work of Irish interest. It is a leader in this field and commands top prices for the work on its shelves.

FRANCIS STREET,
Dublin 8
This street is the closest Dublin comes to possessing an antiques district, with a variety of outlets running down its entire length. Quality varies enormously, but prices are generally high and proprietors more astute than they might appear. The best-known retailer here is Chantal O'Sullivan at 43–44 Francis Street (Tel: 01 4541143). With a second outlet in New York, she tends to specialize in large pieces of 18th- and 19th-century Irish mahogany furniture, along with smaller items such as inlaid wooden boxes and cut-glass decanters.

GREENE'S
16 Clare Street, Dublin 2
Tel: 01 6762554
Just off Merrion Square, this is a charming place in which to idle away half an hour. Greene's is a 19th-century bookshop, with an exterior and interior still intact. Climb the stairs to the seemingly anarchic first floor, where second-hand volumes tumble from the shelves. A section there is devoted to inexpensive copies of work by Irish authors.

THE SILVER SHOP
Powerscourt Townhouse, South William Street, Dublin 2
Tel: 01 6794147
Although there are few practitioners today, in the 18th and 19th centuries Dublin could boast many master silversmiths. Wonderful examples of their workmanship can be found on Ian Haslam's premises, one of a row of antiques outlets located along one side of this aristocratic townhouse's first-floor courtyard. Haslam is highly knowledgeable and happy to discuss Irish silver with interested customers. Haslam also carries a range of fine painted antique miniatures.

WEIR & SONS LTD
96–99 Grafton Street, Dublin 2
Tel: 01 6779678
Weir's is very grand: Dublin's oldest and most prestigious jeweler dating back to the mid-19th century. The shop is still fitted out in Victorian style and offers impeccable service of a similar vintage. Along with watches, leather goods and pens by the most distinguished international marques, the shop also carries a large stock of antique Irish silver.

CRAFTS AND GIFTS

Avoca Handweavers
11–13 Suffolk Street, Dublin 2
Tel: 01 6774215
More an emporium than a shop, Avoca Handweavers is the city-centre outlet for a very successful family business based outside Dublin. Spread over several levels, the store is crammed with everything from women's and children's clothing to bed linen, to take-away food. The top-floor restaurant, offering delicious home-made meals, is deservedly popular and a good choice for Sunday brunch.

Blarney Woollen Mills
21–23 Nassau Street, Dublin 2
Tel: 6710068
The windows of this shop invariably display an assortment of Irish knitwear, so this is certainly the most convenient spot in which to purchase an Aran sweater. But also for sale is a generous selection of tweed and linen clothing for men and women, plus Waterford Crystal and Belleek porcelain.

Claddagh Records
2 Cecilia Street, Dublin 2
Tel: 01 6770262
When admirers of traditional Irish music first began to record old performers and their repertoire, the work was produced by Claddagh, which remains the pre-eminent label in this area. Here can be found the fullest and finest stock of such music in Dublin, along with staff who are both knowledgeable and interested in the subject.

Cleo
18 Kildare Street, Dublin 2
Tel: 01 6761421
Since the 1930s, family-owned Cleo has been supporting Irish weavers and knitters. The shop offers Aran sweaters in every conceivable range and colour, plus gorgeous tweeds made into clothes for men and women. Romantics may wish to buy one of the heavy velvet evening cloaks originally made in Kinsale, County Cork.

Design Yard
12 East Essex Street, Dublin 2
Tel: 01 6778453
Opened in 1993 as a purpose-built showcase for the best in contemporary Irish design, the shop's ground floor is devoted to jewelry, of which specially commissioned exhibitions are regularly held. The upstairs is given over to a more diverse range of products: furniture, accessories, rugs and glassware produced by craftworkers across the country.

The Kilkenny Shop
5–6 Nassau Street, Dublin 2
Tel: 01 6777066
Directly opposite a parking site where tourist buses let off their passengers, the Kilkenny Shop acts as a magnet for these putative spenders. And why not?

When the premises carry so much and all Irish-made: clothing, glassware, pottery, food and household goods. The first floor holds a café and a restaurant, both with extensive and excellent menus.

FOOD AND WINE

Berry Bros & Rudd Ltd
4 Harry Street, Dublin 2
Tel: 01 6773444
An English winemerchant, Berry Bros opened its first Irish outlet in a charming little old building which used to be the government premises for weights and measures. Excellent stock, knowledgeable staff and a delightful interior at a very convenient location off Grafton Street.

Big Cheese Company
St Andrew's Lane, Dublin 2
Tel: 01 6711399
The name gives a good idea of what is stocked here, but aside from cheeses, there is also a wide variety of other delicatessen foodstuffs, a large number of them important from the United States.

Findlater's
The Vaults, Harcourt Street, Dublin 2
Tel: 01 4751699
Findlater's was once the smartest grocers in Dublin After that business closed, one member of the family went into the wine business and opened in these premises a series of vaults under a former railway station. There is not only a substantial choice of wines, beers and spirits on offer, but also a display of memorabilia from the city's retail history.

Irish Yeast Company
6 College Street, Dublin 2
Tel: 01 6778575
Not many people now need yeast, either fresh or dried, but that is not really the purpose of including this shop. Somehow, in the midst of relentless social and commercial upheaval, and despite terrible traffic congestion, it remains quietly trading. It not only has yeast for sale, but all the devices you would need for baking and cake-making.

Mitchell & Son Ltd
21 Kildare Street, Dublin 2
Tel: 01 6760766
There may be an abundance of off-licences now all over Dublin, but Mitchell's is the oldest and smartest of them all. Beautiful premises, fine stock and the kind of discreet, courteous service you simply do not find in more recently opened outlets.

Sawers
3 Chatham Street, Dublin 2
Tel: 01 6777643
An exceptional survivor in the smartest retailing district of Dublin, Sawers is a fishmonger's shop which has been on the same site for many decades. Visitors to the city are unlikely to need fresh cod or

mackerel, but the company's Irish smoked salmon tastes delicious and travels well.

Sheridan Cheesemongers
11 South Anne Street, Dublin 2
Tel: 6793143
Ireland's cheese producers have undergone a renaissance in the past ten years and this is the place to find the results – a small but perfectly contained shop selling the best of the country's produce. Sheridan's is also good for olives, chutneys, relishes and other such food, and carries a range of sandwiches at lunchtime.

MARKETS

Dublin's most famous marketeer, Molly Malone, would be disappointed to discover that relatively little street trading is done today in her native city. Most people now shop in supermarkets, just like everywhere else. However, one long-standing survivor of the tradition is Moore Street, where latter-day Mollies sell fruit and vegetables daily (except Sundays), along with a variety of other goods, depending on the season. The traders here have often inherited pitches which have been in their families for generations and their speech is authentic old-Dublin argot. Moore Street is not particularly smart and, unless you need to stock up on groceries, the only reason for paying a visit is to observe the standholders, who may not necessarily take kindly to such attention while they work.

For a more stylish alternative, Temple Bar's Meeting House Square hosts an open-air market every Saturday. Again, most of the stalls are selling food, but of a wider variety and higher quality than on Moore Street: country cheeses; smoked fish; home-made jams and chutneys. Not far away on Cow's Lane can be found (on Saturdays) a second market that concentrates on organic produce, fruit and vegetables, but also eggs, meat and various dairy products.

In the main Temple Bar Square, a second-hand book fair is held most weekends, but it is a rather small-scale and half-hearted affair. Better to wander to the George's Street Arcade, a covered Victorian market running from Drury Street to South Great George's Street. The range of goods daily available from the shops and stands is enormous – second-hand CDs and books, wine, food, clothing and furniture. Prices are just as varied. In addition, the arcade contains a number of modestly priced cafés.

Several other covered markets in Dublin have closed down over the past few years, but one determined survivor is that in Smithfield off Mary's Lane. One, now rather shabby building just about continues to accommodate a small number of independent fishmongers, but its newly restored neighbour holds lots of traders in fruit, vegetables and flowers. Cognoscenti claim that the best time to visit is in the very early morning – around 6 am – when the best quality and value is to be found. However, there is still an abundance of stock for anyone who rises slightly later in the day.

MUSEUMS

Central Catholic Library
74 Merrion Square, Dublin 2
Tel: 01 6761264
Not strictly speaking a museum, but an endearing remnant of a Dublin otherwise entirely vanished. In a handsome 18th-century house, the century-old library is open to the general public ,but is usually very quiet. Take time out to browse among the tightly packed bookshelves in which works of a religious nature inevitably predominate.

Chester Beatty Library
Clock Tower Building, Dublin Castle, Dame Street, Dublin 2
Tel: 01 4070750
Awarded the accolade of European Museum of the Year in 2002, the Chester Beatty Library moved to its present premises only 18 months earlier. Its contents were collected by the wealthy Anglo-American mining magnate, Sir Alfred Chester Beatty, who bequeathed his estate to the Irish nation in 1969. The range of items on display is truly remarkable: Islamic illuminated manuscripts, ancient Egyptian papyri, Greek Orthodox and Coptic icons, Japanese Samurai armour. There are also temporary exhibitions, in addition to the permanent display.

Dublin Civic Museum
58 South William Street, Dublin 2
Tel: 01 6794260
This delightful 18th-century building, which once housed the city's Assembly Rooms, is now home to a museum filled with rescued artifacts from its past. An excellent way to understand the history of Dublin, thanks to a judicious selection of items and images, such as James Malton's famous prints of the capital, first produced in 1790s. Temporary exhibitions are regularly arranged.

Dublin Writers' Museum
18–19 Parnell Square, Dublin 1
Tel: 01 8722077
The city's literary history is so rich that it makes sense to have a museum dedicated to Dublin's writers. The enormous building in which it is housed deserves to be seen, especially the very grand first-floor reception rooms. While some of the material is a little thin, this is an excellent introduction to Irish literature for those not overly familiar with the subject.

Hugh Lane Municipal Gallery of Modern Art
Charlemont House, Parnell Square North, Dublin 1
Tel: 01 8741903
The Earl of Charlemont built this miniature palace as his Dublin townhouse in 1762 and some 170 years later it was converted into a museum to hold the collection of modern art, originally assembled by dealer/collector Sir Hugh Lane. Among the most important assets are the Barbizon and Impressionist pictures and, the venue's latest acquisition, Francis Bacon's studio installed on the premises in 2001.

Mountjoy Sq

2

Nth Grt George St

7

12

13

Parnell Sq E

35

27

Parnell Sq W

Moore Street

O'Connell Street

St Mary's
Pro-Cathedral

Parnell Street

14

Custom
House

8

Morning Star Ave.

National Museum
of Ireland

33   23

Capel Street

29

Bachelors Walk

22

3

Liffey

11

Ormond Quay

Temple Bar

Four
Courts

Essex Qy   34

1

Westmorland St

D'Olier St

College St

Guinness Brewery

Trinity College
The Book of Kells

College Park

25

28

4

5

Dublin Castle
St Werburgh's Church

Grafton St

Nassau Street

Leinster St Sth

Clare St

24

26

6

South Grt George's St

Grafton Street

Dawson Street

Kildare Street

19

18

15

20   21

32   10

Merrion St Upper West

North

17

South

East

30

16

West

North

Merrion Row

Fitzwilliam Lane

Baggot Street

Fitz. St Lwr

St Stephen's
Green

East

South

Wexford   Camden Street Lower

Newman
House

9

University
College

Fitzwilliam East

Fitzwilliam St Upper

31

Charlemont St

IRISH MUSEUM OF MODERN ART
Royal Hospital, Military Road, Kilmainham, Dublin 8
Tel: 01 6129900

The largest extant complex of 17th-century buildings in Ireland, the Royal Hospital was constructed in 1684 as the equivalent of Les Invalides in Paris. In 1991, after many years of neglect it was converted into a national museum of modern art. Whether suitable for this purposes or not, the venue does its best to give visitors a sense of what is happening in contemporary art both within Ireland and overseas. In any case, the Royal Hospital deserves to be seen if only for its restored baroque gardens and exuberantly decorated chapel.

JAMES JOYCE CULTURAL CENTRE
35 North Great George's Street, Dublin 1
Tel: 01 8788547

A whole building dedicated to just one writer. Yet such is the global interest in Joyce, that the place is constantly busy. The property, which in Joyce's time housed a dance academy, now houses a substantial library containing early editions and texts of the various works, plus a wide variety of Joyceana, certain to interest admirers. They will probably also want to visit a second Joyce Museum found in an old martello tower where he (briefly) lived at Sandycove on the south Dublin coastline (Tel: 01 2809265).

KILMAINHAM GAOL
Inchicore Road, Kilmainham, Dublin 8
Tel: 01 4535984

Dating from the last years of the 18th century, this gaol was where successive generations of Irish opponents to the British government were imprisoned, including the participants in the Easter 1916 Rising, who were executed on the premises. It must have been a grim place then and is scarcely cheerful now as a museum, but definitely worth visiting in order to gain a better understanding of Ireland's troubled history.

NATIONAL GALLERY OF IRELAND
Merrion Square West, Dublin 2
Tel: 01 6615133

Founded in 1854, the NGI has an excellent and representative collection of European art from the 14th to the 20th centuries. But what will most interest overseas visitors is the extensive display of Irish painting, since the native school is little known outside of the country. Irish art only really started to develop its own identity in the 18th century and, as might be expected, landscape has always been a strong genre. An impressive new extension to the gallery opened in early 2002 with room for large temporary exhibitions.

NATIONAL LIBRARY OF IRELAND
(AND HERALDIC MUSEUM)
Kildare Street, Dublin 2
Tel: 01 6030200

Although most of the building operates as a research library, the handsome 19th-century entrance hall hosts a constant series of exhibitions covering a wide range of subjects, often relating to aspects of Irish history. There is also a genealogical service for visitors wishing to research their family history and, further down Kildare Street, the National Library is also responsible for the Heraldic Museum, where information relating to Irish clans can be discovered.

NATIONAL MUSEUM OF IRELAND
Kildare Street, Dublin 2 and Collins Barracks, Benburb Street, Dublin 3
Tel: 01 6777444

The need for greater space to display its treasures has led the National Museum to be divided between two premises on either side of the city. In the original city-centre building can be seen the remarkable metalwork produced in Ireland in pre- and early Christian times, along with many other archaeological finds. Meanwhile, in what were once the largest military barracks in Europe, the museum has installed its collections relating to the decorative arts and Irish history. Among the exhibitions of special interest are those covering silver and glass, furniture and fashion, and the personal archive of the Irish-born, 20th-century designer Eileen Gray.

NATURAL HISTORY MUSEUM
Merrion Street Upper, Dublin 2
Tel: 01 6777444

The Natural History Museum gives the impression of being almost entirely untouched since it first opened to the public in 1857 and this is the reason why an opportunity to visit the place should not be overlooked. It is an almost unique example of Victorian culture. Delightful old-fashioned displays of Irish flora and fauna.

THE OLD LIBRARY
Trinity College, Dublin 2
Tel: 01 6082308

Perhaps the most beautiful building in Trinity College, the Old Library was first constructed in the opening years of the 18th century. Its barrel-vaulted first-floor Long Room, more than 200 feet long, used to be where the Book of Kells, the finest illuminated manuscript in Ireland, was displayed. The work is now shown in another part of the library, along with a number of other medieval religious manuscripts also owned by the college.

ROYAL IRISH ACADEMY
19 Dawson Street, Dublin 2
Tel: 01 6762570

Founded in 1785 in order to encourage the study of 'Science, Polite Literature and Antiquities', the RIA is housed in an elegant 18th-century building with a fine library. This is open to the public and frequently shows exhibitions drawn from the academy's own rich holdings.

BIBLIOGRAPHY

Bennett, Douglas, *Encyclopaedia of Dublin*, Dublin, 1991

Brady, Joseph and Simms, Anngret (eds), *Dublin Through Space and Time (c.900–1900)*, Dublin, 2001

Clarke, H.B. (ed.), *Medieval Dublin: The Making of a Metropolis*, Blackrock, 1990

Conlin, S., *Historic Dublin*, Dublin, 1986

Cosgrave, Dillon, *North Dublin: City and Environs*, Dublin, 1977

Costello, Peter, *Dublin Churches*, Dublin, 1989

Costello, Peter, *Dublin Castle in the Life of the Irish Nation*, Dublin, 1999

Cowell, John, *Dublin's Famous People and Where they Lived*, Dublin, 1980

Craig, Julie (compiler), *See Dublin on Foot: An Architectural Walking Guide*, Dublin, 2001

Craig, Maurice, *Dublin 1660–1860*, Dublin, 1980

De Courcy, J.W., *The Liffey in Dublin*, Dublin, 1996

Devlin, Polly, *Dublin*, London, 1993

Fagan, P., *The Second City: Portrait of Dublin 1700–60*, Dublin, 1986

Gillespie, Elgy (ed.), *The Liberties of Dublin*, Dublin, 1973

Gorham, M., *Dublin from Old Photographs*, London, 1972

Guinness, Desmond, *Georgian Dublin*, London, 1979

Kelly, Deirdre, *Four Roads to Dublin*, Dublin, 1995

McDonald, Frank, *The Construction of Dublin*, Cork, 2000

Maxwell, Constantia, *Dublin under the Georges 1714–1830*, Dublin, 1997

McCullough, Niall, *Dublin: An Urban History*, Dublin, 1989

McCullough, Niall, *A Vision of the City: Dublin and the Wide Streets Commissioners*, Dublin, 1991

Norris, David, *Joyce's Dublin*, Dublin, 1982

O'Brien, Jacqueline and Guiness, Desmond, *Dublin: A Grand Tour*, London, 1994

O'Dwyer, Frederick, *Lost Dublin*, Dublin, 1981

Pakenham, Thomas and Valerie (eds), *Dublin: A Traveller's Companion*, London, 1988

Pritchett, V.S., *Dublin: A Portrait*, London, 1967

Somerville-Large, Peter, *Dublin*, London, 1979

Williams, Jeremy, *Architecture in Ireland 1837–1921*, Dublin, 1994

Text © 2003 Robert O'Byrne
Photographs © Alex Ramsay

Library of Congress Catalog Card Number 2003100800
ISBN 0-500-51132-2

First published in hardcover in the United States of America in 2003 by Thames & Hudson Inc., 500 Fifth Avenue, New York, New York 10110

thamesandhudsonusa.com

Printed and bound in China by Midas Printing